# City Politics and the Press

# City Politics and
# the Press

## Journalists and the Governing of
## Merseyside

### Harvey Cox
Lecturer in Politics
University of Liverpool

### David Morgan
Lecturer in American Government and Politics
University of Liverpool

Cambridge
at the University Press
1973

Published by the Syndics of the Cambridge University Press
Bentley House, 200 Euston Road, London NW1 2DB
American Branch: 32 East 57th Street, New York, N.Y. 10022

Library of Congress Catalogue Card Number: 72–96678

ISBN: 0 521 20162 4

Printed in Great Britain by
Western Printing Services Ltd, Bristol

# Contents

*List of Tables*                                    *page* vi

*Preface*                                                vii

1   Introduction                                           1
2   The local press in Britain                             5
3   Theoretical considerations                            16
4   Merseyside in the 1960s                               34
5   Press content analysed                                46
6   What the papers said: case histories                 73
7   Editorial perspectives                               110
8   The press and local politicians                      124
9   Conclusion                                           131

*Notes*                                                  151

*Select bibliography*                                    155

*Index*                                                  158

# Tables

1   Circulation of classes of newspaper in Great Britain     5

2   Functional analysis of mass communications     19

3   Party strengths on councils (councillors and aldermen), 1962–69     41

4   Categories of news coverage     48

5   Total content by type (column-inches) (5 per cent sample; 1962–69 inclusive)     55

6   Total coverage of local government and politics, 1962–69     57

7   Newspaper coverage of services common to all, by functional category     58

8   Coverage of selected services, by functional category, (%) 1962–69     60

9   Local government services – rank order of coverage and coverage groups     67

10   Ratio of large to small mentions     68

11   Year by year selected service coverage (mentions) (three newspapers)     70

12   Editors and service coverage     118

# Preface

We are glad to acknowledge the debts we owe to a number of people. Our general indebtedness to those who have written on the study of communication, and especially of the press, is clear from our text. We valued the advice and assistance of our colleagues Professor F. F. Ridley, Dr Noel Boaden, and Mr Henry Finch; and that of Professor Joe Banks now at Leicester University. We cannot omit to express our gratitude to the journalists of the Merseyside press whose interest was most encouraging and whose opinion we value.

The privilege of our errors must, of course, be reserved for us.

Liverpool                                                         Harvey Cox
October 1972                                                 David Morgan

TO

B. and S.

# 1

# Introduction

> A newspaper . . . is much more than a business; it is an
> institution; it reflects and it influences the life of a whole
> community; it may affect even wider destinies. It is, in its way,
> an instrument of government.
>
> C. P. Scott, *The Manchester Guardian*, May 1921

Although the local press clearly has a unique place in the life of
the community its investigation, to date, has been slight. Opinions
might well differ as to the sense in which local newspapers may be
regarded as instruments of government; but it is hardly in dispute
that the press holds a central position in the relationship between the
governed and the governors.

The Research Report on the Local Government Elector which was
carried out for the Maud Committee on the Management of Local
Government attempted to uncover the sources and character of
popular perceptions of local government. The local newspaper, it
was asserted, is 'the biggest vehicle of communication for local
government'.[1] The survey revealed that 79 per cent of the electorate
claim to be regular readers of local newspapers, with another 10 per
cent reading them irregularly. In the county boroughs the 'regular'
total was as high as 84 per cent. When asked the source of information of 'the local news item most recently heard' (of those who had
heard any news of their local council in the previous month) 68 per
cent nominated the local paper as that source, compared with only
11 per cent for the next largest category, those who had heard it
'by word of mouth' from friends, neighbours or workmates. The
Skeffington Committee[2] noted that 'we have no doubt that the local
press provides one of the vital means of publicity open to a local
planning authority. It achieves enormous coverage; something
approaching 90 per cent of the adult population are likely to read
at least one local newspaper, and, so far as the authority is concerned, such publicity is free.' In their search for means of increasing
public participation in planning, the Committee assigned press
publicity a vital role. 'Publicity alone', they comment, 'is not
participation; but it is the first essential step towards it.'

While the Research Report's figures on local newspaper *penetration* into households are impressive, the Report also produces evidence which casts grave doubt on the *effectiveness* of the press, at least at present, in the local political communication process. Only 30 per cent of the sample interviewed said they had heard anything at all about their council in the last month. Only one in four of those who claimed to be regular local newspaper readers were able to recall a news item about the local council. Tests of ability to mention any of nine selected local authority services revealed that, amongst all informants, the refuse collection service was the best known, while 20 per cent of people were unable to name any at all. Only 28 per cent of informants were able to name the mayor or chairman of their local authority. 65 per cent of the sample of electors in county boroughs felt they did not 'know enough about what the council is doing to make full use of their services', while 61 per cent agreed they didn't 'know enough to know whether they are doing the right things for me or not'. Councillors' views on the public indicated that they felt the same, only more so. For instance, 78 per cent of councillors in county boroughs agreed that 'the public does not know enough to get a balanced picture of the way the council conducts its affairs'.[3]

The Research Report comments that 'if the local newspapers are indeed seen as regularly as electors claim, then the local council news items they contain do not make a very lasting impression on those who are exposed to them . . . only a minority at present seems to have found a way of absorbing at least some of the relevant information which must appear in the local press.'[4]

Many reasons might account for this situation. Most people are weakly motivated to learn about local government. The system itself, as many commentators have emphasised, is highly confusing to many people, and it would be unfair to fault the press for failures of perception of a system widely regarded as ill-adapted to both contemporary needs and democratic aspirations. If people are weakly motivated towards taking an interest in the running of their affairs locally, we may say there has been something wrong with our present ways of ordering our local affairs, or that there is something lacking in the country's political culture, or again that it was unreasonable for a complex of reasons ever to have expected otherwise. Nor need we necessarily endorse the widely held assumption that the public *ought* to be less indifferent. But the lack of accord between the evidence of, on the one hand, extremely poor knowledge of local government and, on the other, the widespread penetration of local newspapers amongst the electorate, suggests a cluster of problems which require investigation. What do people look for in their local paper? This would be a study in itself, being a part of the problem of mass perceptions in general. But we can ask what readers actually find on the printed page. How much, and of what kind, is the coverage given to local government and politics? In what ways does the press act to process information and, on its own part, to lead or stimulate its readers' political awareness? Under what constraints does the press operate? How does the journalist see his role? How far is he aware of choice in his operations? How do local political leaders and activists see the paper and its producers? The answers to these questions, if they could be obtained, would illuminate this dark area of our knowledge of local politics and of the media in Britain, and would enable us to assess in some measure the scope for change in the quality of local democracy through the press.

Apart from the evidence in the Maud Committee's Research Reports, and isolated scraps of other evidence, there is little or no existing information on the role played by the local newspaper in the local political system in Britain. The few studies of British community politics which have appeared, such as those of Glossop,[5] Newcastle under Lyme[6] or Sheffield,[7] have given the local press very little attention. Studies of public political communication in Britain have also neglected this field, looking at the parties' means of influencing voters,[8] the effects of television on political understanding,[9] and the relationship of the national press to politics,[10] but ignoring local political communication. A recent valuable study by Ian Jackson of the provincial press[11] devotes considerable attention to the press as purveyor of consensual attitudes on social and political affairs and, importantly, demonstrates the general political partisanship of the press. These are important contributions; but since his approach is not that of a political scientist it follows that most of the questions posed above – especially the issue of how much and what kind of coverage is given to local politics – are left unanswered.

The present study is aimed at just these questions. We are concerned to examine the local press – in its key aspects – and to analyse its actual coverage. We begin by examining the relation of the local press to the provincial and national press – as a business and, particularly, as a communications business. There follows a discussion of aspects of communications theory which, *inter alia*, is aimed at suggesting a fruitful method of analysis of press coverage of local politics. Together these chapters enable us to see the press as a number of profit-seeking institutions performing important communication roles.

Then in chapter 4 we turn to the local press on Merseyside, a not untypical collection of weeklies and dailies in a conurbation setting. First we examine the social, political and economic setting of these newspapers, and then the papers themselves. There follows an analysis of their coverage of local politics in the 1960s – chapter 5 – and an analysis of the kind of coverage given to a selection of policy and 'news' areas. We thus form a picture, not only of how much local political news the papers of one conurbation provided, but also of its character.

Bearing in mind the situation of the local press in general, and the specific case of Merseyside, we then look at those who produce the papers and some of their most avid readers. In chapter 7 we examine the view of the world as seen from the editor's chair. In chapter 8 we look at the attitudes towards the press of some of those most directly affected by its coverage – a sample of party officers and councillors. Finally, we try to draw conclusions on the nature of press coverage, what changes might be possible and, not least, what kinds of changes would be desirable.

# 2

# The local press in Britain

The local newspaper has been regarded as something of a Cinderella of the press world, and has been neglected by students. Circulation figures, however, suggest that the local press deserves attention. As indicated in Table 1, circulation of local weeklies and bi-weeklies is almost as great as of the national morning papers, while the local paper achieves even greater significance if the 'provincial evenings'

Table 1. *Circulation of classes of newspaper in Great Britain*[1]

|  | National morning | Provincial morning | Provincial evening | Weeklies and bi-weekly |
|---|---|---|---|---|
| 1937 | 9,980,000 | 1,600,000 | 4,400,000 | 8,572,000 |
| 1966 | 15,635,000 | 1,954,000 | 6,824,000 | 13,825,000 |
| 1969 | 14,804,000 | 1,973,000 | 6,889,000 | 13,423,000 |

are included in the reckoning. The actual numbers of papers are subject to constant fluctuation, but at the end of 1970 there were 1,179 weeklies and 103 provincial daily papers in the United Kingdom, all but 17 of them evenings. Between 1962 and 1964 six cities lost one of their evening papers – Birmingham, Edinburgh, Leeds, Leicester, Manchester and Nottingham – so that in 1970 only in Glasgow and London was there a choice of evening paper. In the case of the first three categories of paper, circulation showed a steady rise to a peak in 1957, but has fallen off since then. The national morning papers, indeed, have lost one million in circulation since 1957. There are fewer of them than in 1945, and the financial difficulties of many are well known. The weeklies and bi-weeklies, however, have shown no such falling off of circulation. Several have disappeared but several new ones have been successfully launched. Indeed, it may be claimed that the local press has benefited more than most sections of the press from changes in organisation and methods of production during the 1950s and 1960s. Typographical improvements have made many more visually attractive than they were even ten years ago. Computer assistance and other techniques has made typesetting less laborious. Thus the local press has been

5

able to appear in more attractive formats, with clear print and photographs, better quality paper and bolder layout, and also by and large, to cope with the inevitable spiralling of costs. The method of photolithographic printing, known as web-offset, has been an important factor in the case of papers of a certain size, particularly those with limited, predictable 'runs', i.e. the smaller papers. The local paper, for the first time, is capable of bearing comparison, for attractiveness and readability, with the best that the national press can offer.

Circulation figures also indicate the relative weakness of the position of the provincial morning papers. None has a circulation of more than 130,000. Their growth in circulation has been very considerably less than those of the other categories of paper, while rising costs have forced a number out altogether, and compelled the others to use more popular local papers as props.

It is known that papers reach far more people than actually buy them. The Institute of Practitioners in Advertising estimates that three times the number of people who buy a paper actually read one. Unfortunately, their surveys do not cover the provincial or local press but, at the national level, they believe that 50 per cent of people see more than one paper daily.[2] The readership of the provincial evening newspapers as estimated by the Evening Newspaper Advertising Bureau in 1969 is particularly high. Generally, in the cities proper, these newspapers are taken by over three-quarters of the households. In terms of social class the readership is proportionately slightly more working than middle class, a margin which increases as one moves from the south to the north of England. The reverse is true in the case of the weekly paper which, generally, is more widely taken in the south than the north and by a larger proportion of the middle classes as one moves south.[3]

The more 'local' a paper is, the greater the probability of its readers having read other papers at other 'levels', and that this will form an element in the overall context in which the local paper is viewed by its readers. But we are unable to say what degrees of overlap are involved. It would, in particular, be useful to know what proportion of readers of provincial morning and evening papers are readers of other local papers, such as weeklies, operating within the circulation area of the former. The Chester edition of the *Liverpool Echo*, for example, goes into a quarter of the homes of Chester. Chester is unusually well covered in that it also has a weekly of its own and is the centre for another paper largely circulating in the county of Cheshire. Such papers may reinforce, merely duplicate, or actually contradict each other in the surveillance which they offer of political life in general, or of specific local issues. Any study of the potential impact of political coverage would obviously be the sharper for information on who reads what. We do know from the Maud Research (*inter alia*) that a local paper of some sort is claimed to be read by around 80 per cent of the population. But we have no means of checking the reality behind this claim, or the breakdown of readership by age, sex and social class as it applies to particular papers. Again the readership profile of the provincial morning paper, the paper with the most problematic circulation, would be most valuable for this kind of assessment.

The numbers of journalists on provincial newspapers (United Kingdom except Scotland) increased by some 1,000 to a total of around 8,500 in 1968.[4] The increase was probably due, says the National Union of Journalists, to the increase in numbers of pages, arising, in turn, from increased flows of advertising business. Of the 8,500, about 55 per cent worked in the 63 provincial daily newspaper offices in England, Wales and Belfast, the other 45 per cent in the 228 weekly offices. These figures indicate straight away the immense difference between the scale of operations of the provincial daily and the weekly. Moreover, the ratio of juniors to senior journalists is much greater on the weeklies than on the dailies, a disparity which increased during the 1960s. It is clear that the weeklies have functioned as training grounds for the journalistic profession at large. The Newspaper Society and the National Union of Journalists have attempted to persuade daily papers to take on more of this work so as to relieve the weeklies of overmanning by juniors. But the situation is not improved by the fact that many weeklies and dailies are under the same proprietors, who find it profitable to run the former on apprentice and junior labour.

Throughout the 1960s the annual turnover of labour was between 15 per cent and 20 per cent. In 1968, the provincial newspaper industry lost 139 who left journalism and 245 who died, retired or emigrated. This represented 4·6 per cent of total manpower. A similar percentage was lost to other sections of journalism. Of 402 who left the provincial papers for other branches of the journalistic profession in 1968, 125 were recruited by the national press and the London evenings; 69 moved into public relations,

55 to the news agencies, 38 to radio and television. The rest went into other miscellaneous journalistic posts. While the largest single category of junior journalists leaving their papers for known causes was that of those who left journalism altogether, the national press and the London evenings took the largest single group among the more senior men. Overall, London took 7 per cent of the turnover. But even more striking was the 26·5 per cent represented by the provincial daily papers. Some of this consisted of men and women who moved from one provincial daily to another, but a high proportion was made up of recruitment by the provincial dailies from the weeklies.

It can be inferred, then, that the provincial weekly paper is the milch-cow of the national newspaper industry, as far as manpower is concerned. It trains most of the incomers to the profession, only to lose many of the best of them. At the other end, not all good journalists go to London. But every year, it exacts its tribute of talent.

Each year too, it seems, London comes nearer the provincial journalist. The 1960s were years not only of newspaper closure, but also of managerial mergers and, increasingly, of steady advance in multiple ownership by London-based newspaper chains. By 1969 over half of the English and Welsh provincial evening newspapers were in the hands of five London-based groups – News of the World Organisation Ltd., Associated Newspapers, United Newspapers, the Thomson Organisation and the Westminster Press Group. The bulk of those papers were in small- to medium-sized cities – the big city evenings were in other hands. The weeklies showed in the 1960s a similar trend. In 1961 the five groups controlled just over 11·2 per cent of them, by 1964 perhaps 18 per cent, and by the end of 1969 over 20 per cent.[5] The provincial morning papers are the stablemates of successful evening papers which are themselves independent of the chains, and the nuclei of smallish groups themselves. According to George Viner, the provincial mornings 'are maintained because they provide a protection against intrusion into the circulation area, carry their share of potential overheads, and offer some potential for the future'.[6] He suggests that they are trying to move into the 'quality' field as regional papers exploiting a national trend. But it is an open question how long the attempt to build on prestige and regional status will maintain these papers. Meanwhile, their losses are made up by their stablemates.

The question of losses is vital, for whatever else they may be, newspapers are businesses seeking profits through the acquisition and dissemination of information. Their capacity to 'act as an information source', as Dilys Hill has pointed out, is affected by the way they are 'owned and managed'.[7] The process of acquisition of information involves the selling of space to individual and business advertisers, and the acquiring of new information of personal, social, political or economic interest. The process of dissemination involves the sale of copies of the newspaper. This in turn involves the finding and keeping of a market, i.e. purchasers, some of whose needs the paper is prepared to meet and go on meeting satisfactorily. The newspaper, to continue in business as a profitable enterprise, must do two things. First, it must sell space, from which comes most of its revenue. Secondly, it must retain reader-interest in order to sell copies so as in turn to make itself attractive to advertisers wishing to reach large numbers of people.

Advertising revenue is a far more significant contribution to income than sales. Hence readership is a more vital consideration to newspapermen than circulation.[8] Revenue comes roughly in the proportion one-third sales, two-thirds advertising. With weekly papers the advertising proportion goes up to 80 per cent. Of the latter about half is classified, i.e. local, individual and domestic. Advertising revenue is thus a compensation for heavy loss on the cover price of the paper. It is, inevitably, sensitive to the state of the economy. The economic squeeze of 1966–8 lowered newspaper profit margins and led to strenuous newspaper campaigns to ensure more and new sources of advertisements of all kinds. The loss to television advertisements in the 1950s and 1960s had been, in the words of John Goulden, 'more than recouped from the increase in classified advertising'.[9] The campaign for more revenue led, as he describes, to high-pressure sales efforts and improved organisation inside the paper to deal with the mass of new copy received.[10] The viability of the press in the late 1960s, he notes, 'owed much to the growth of classified advertising'.[11]

Newspaper owners and editors *as* businessmen must know their market and gauge that mix of information which will give them a viable level of profit. Basically this means that they must balance what is commonly called 'news' with advertisements. The cost to the newspaper of advertising is more than borne by the advertisers. The cost to the newspaper of providing 'news' of all kinds is somewhat recouped from sales of the paper and the generation of more advertisements. But those in the news do not pay to be in the press except where, as in the case of some local authorities, they employ public relations officers and staffs. The imperatives of the newspaper are clear. It will find itself seeking to maximise advertising at the same time as it seeks to provide 'news' which will ensure constant or growing sales, in turn to ensure its advertising income.

Knowing the market, then, is crucial to all newspapers – national, provincial or local. The owners and editors of all three know that their product not only competes with other media but also, to differing degrees, with other newspapers. Each caters for different expectations and, insofar as it succeeds as a business, may be regarded as largely a product of these expectations. What is the situation of the local newspaper as a medium of local communication?

The audience of the local town weekly paper is significantly different in kind from that of the national paper, with, perhaps, that of the provincial metropolitan daily lying somewhere in between them. There is, in mass communications, as McQuail puts it, a 'massness continuum'[12] in which we may place at one end the great London-based television organisations, and, near to the other, the small local newspaper. Several factors will differentiate the latter from the former. The audience for the local newspaper will be less heterogeneous, as national differences of class, region or occupation are modified into the specific pattern of the local area, in which some of the range of differences within the nation may be of comparatively little account. The very homogeneity of his audience may itself produce pressures on the local communicator. The relationship between him and his audience is likely to be less anonymous than is the case with national media. He may well be part of the same social networks as a high proportion of his key sources and of many of the people whose activities it is his job to scrutinise and report. He may thus have patronage, in terms of publicity, to distribute amongst people who are his personal friends and adversaries. On the other hand, he may have personal social losses to sustain by printing news or comment they may dislike. The newspaper as business may also suffer from the consequences of such behaviour.

Bureaucratisation, hierarchy and division of function are more fully developed in the organisation of national mass media than in the provincial daily, or the small local. At the extreme, perhaps, we may cite the small town proprietor–editor running what is virtually a one-man business. Most local papers are some way from this state, but their organisation is far less complex than those of Fleet Street.

Such is the continuum that it would be mistaken to assume that newspapers operating at different national levels are strongly in competition with each other. The local weekly paper and the metropolitan daily are unlikely to compete except in the sense that as commercial enterprises they are both subject to economic conditions. A price increase on the part of the latter may well result in a fall in the circulation of the former, as readers decide which is the more dispensable. But, in general, they provide a somewhat different focus of interest for their readers. A series of weeklies operating under the umbrella of the large metropolitan daily cannot replicate the latter's services, but must seek to play the distinct role of providing information about *local* residents, *local* issues, *local* neighbourhood organisations etc.

There is a range of variation from the purely 'local' paper. Not only is there the provincial daily, product of an organisation much closer to the Fleet Street pattern, but also the local weekly which is not locally owned but is part of a larger group, as many have become in recent years. Hence there is often a combination of comparatively modest local operations on the editorial side with a more elaborate general finance and policy structure centralised elsewhere. Frequently the provincial morning and evening paper tend to compliment each other. The evening paper, a more recent development in the industry, tends to have more of the character of a 'popular' paper, i.e. to be more personal, less 'solid' in presentation, with more human interest and entertainment features. It may also be more exclusively urban (circulating within the inner circulation area of the morning paper), and has the greatest penetration. Most of those who read it may be pictured as 'unwinding' after the main work of the day. The main national and international news of the day may well be already known. Finally, a high proportion of evening papers are direct offshoots of the morning paper and are produced in the same office, to a degree by the same men. The provincial morning paper, however, may well be in competition with the national morning press, a situation reflected in their attempt to provide surveillance of the international, national and local scenes all in one paper. That they are subject to a squeeze from both ends may be evidenced by the fact that in many cases they rely, as we noted, on their offshoot evening paper for financial support.

Market opportunities interact with resources and reporting capacity, past and present, to produce newspapers. The national papers and the provincial dailies employ a specialised staff of reporters and correspondents who can, and do, build up a store of expertise and, above all, valuable contacts. The very size and heterogeneity of their 'beats', however, mean that they must spread themselves thinly. Moreover the spread of chain ownership, and general economic pressures have tended to force such papers to keep the numbers of these expensive, senior journalists as low as possible, and to dilute their ranks with younger, less experienced men.

At the level of the local press these tendencies are even more pronounced. Group ownership and centralisation of control have tended to reduce the number of journalists available so that, on a provincial daily, one man might cover several towns or areas of news.[13] He might also, inside the group, help with the coverage provided by the weeklies of each of these towns. Inside these weeklies, as will be seen, the editor is quite likely to be an ex-senior reporter from one of the group's dailies who often has, naturally enough, ambition to return to a more senior position on his former newspaper. This, in itself, need be no bad thing since he is likely to be encouraged to make his paper as attractive and saleable a paper as possible. It may not, however, make for the building up of trustworthy local contacts and, occasionally, in the somewhat parochial world of local politics, may cause resentment. Again, the realities of group life will mean that an editor will consider himself lucky if he has a senior reporter or two and adequate numbers of junior reporters. The bulk of the written material which comes to them in the form of Minutes, Agendas and Reports is not always quickly digestible, serving, as Dilys Hill points out, 'administrative not journalistic ends'.[14] Further, given their staffing problems and situation, they are ill-equipped to be an investigatory press since, as the same author notes, 'they lack specialised staff with time and status to lobby'.[15] Alan Beith, in his study of Banbury newspapers, made the same point, adding that the papers have to rely on local reports and news agencies.[16] Where their own reporters show any promise they will soon be off to the dailies in their own or some other group.

The limited resources of the weeklies or, for that matter, the provincial dailies when covering highly local news is made worse by the complications of access to local government news, *per se.*

Up to 1961 admission of the press to council meetings was governed by the Local Authorities (Admission of the Press to Meetings) Act of 1908. This gave power to full councils to exclude the press where confidential matters were under discussion. The Local Government Act of 1933, which formalised the delegation of council powers to committees, did not modify the 1908 Act, so that the press were wholly excluded. Attempts to modify this in 1931, 1949 and 1950 all failed. The Public Bodies (Admission of the Press to Meetings) Act of 1960 – known as the Thatcher Act after its sponsor, Mrs M. Thatcher (Conservative, Finchley) – secured some change in the legal situation and the climate of public opinion. Previously, the 'abuse' from the press viewpoint had been that council meetings wishing to exclude them simply turned themselves into a committee. The Act – amended in the Commons largely to mollify Labour opposition to open committees – prevented councils doing this. For the smaller councils, where committees normally took in all members, this opened to the press – theoretically – all their meetings. The Act also guaranteed entry into Education Committees, tried to ensure that journalists would be given not merely agendas but some documents relevant to business, and, when they were excluded, a description of the outline of business to be taken. It also extended further the scope of the 'qualified privilege' for comment under which journalists worked.[17] The Defamation Act of 1952 had not, in the eyes of journalists, given them adequate protection. The Thatcher Act is in fact still not considered satisfactory in this respect.

To prevent greater access, many smaller councils responded by dropping one or two members when they went into committee, thus evading the Act and keeping their press out. In the 1960s there was a slow opening of committee meetings to the press. However, research done for the Maud Committee on the Management of Local Government 1967 showed that only a small minority of authorities allowed the press into all their committee meetings (10 per cent), while half allowed no access at all, the London boroughs being notable for this.[18] Despite the Thatcher Act and the strongly worded circular from the Ministry of Housing and Local Government[19] urging greater access, and despite the appeals of successive Ministers, progress has not been very rapid. Speaking in 1965, Richard Crossman M.P., the then Minister, urged greater access to committees, more circulation of material, greater freedom for the press to comment in advance, and better trained journalists. Anthony

Greenwood, speaking in 1969 when holding the same portfolio, urged that councils should honour the Thatcher Act 'in the spirit as well as the letter'.[20]

Crossman's reference to the circulation of material – agendas, minutes, reports etc. – calls attention to another area of press limitation. Committee decisions have to be ratified in full council and are not, of course, binding until this takes place. In consequence, although most council agendas are available to the press before council meetings,[21] too often they miss getting into the weeklies prior to the meeting when comment and public discussion would be possible. Further, even when the agenda *is* available to the weekly prior to going to press, chief officers are often constrained in discussing committee decisions prior to the meeting of the full council. The Royal Commission on the Press, 1947–9, found that nearly a half of local authorities put an embargo on any public reference to committee decisions until the council had met. Alan Beith cites the case of Salford, where the council tried to punish the *Salford City Reporter* for breaking such an embargo.[22] Dilys Hill quoted one of the grounds for this reluctance – a Town Clerk who held that discussion 'would be unfair to those councillors who were not members of the committee concerned'.[23]

The overall results are predictable. Where no embargo exists, and the press deadlines can be met, the press can and does publish some committee decisions – usually with the prefix 'X Committee decided to recommend'. Too often, however, the press finds itself publishing local authority decisions after they have been taken in full council, i.e. when they already have force of law. The dilemmas inherent in the situation are, perhaps, most obvious in the area of planning, but exist in every area of government, and at every level. The citizen may legitimately feel that his democratic rights are reduced to the right to protest *after* the decision is taken, and not *before*, when he might have contributed.

The 1960s, then, witnessed a considerable degree of change in the business and journalistic situation of the local and provincial press. Technical changes, the drive for more advertising and sales, the heavy dependence on junior staff and sometimes rapid staff turn-over, all helped mould the local paper. The concentration of ownership and control in fewer hands also presented a change whose effect is still not easy to assess.

In defence of monopoly it must be acknowledged that, under present conditions, it might be difficult to run as many papers without the economics of some sort of joint operation, and that the career structure afforded may present better opportunities for good journalists. But with a monopoly in news presentation a certain uniformity of basic attitudes to politics is almost inevitable. If it is unavoidable that the local public sees only what the press chooses to let them see of local issues then rivalry in what is presented might at least ensure a measure of illumination and enhance democratic debate.

# 3

# Theoretical considerations

Clearly, if we are to understand the society in which we live we must attempt to explore and theorise about the ways in which we communicate with each other. Students of the social sciences have paid increasing attention to the problems of philosophy, sociology and psychology which underlie the messages which we transmit to each other in person, through our culture, and through our institutions, including those which have been specifically developed as media of communication. This attention is justified, and for two reasons. Communication should have a key place in any models of man or of society which we may be striving to create and refine. And the understanding of communication processes and structures is a necessary preliminary to any effort we might make at improving our social relationships and institutions.

The student of politics is vitally concerned in these activities. A flow of information and opinion takes place between citizens, between political élites, and between the governors and the governed. We cannot comprehend what happens in politics without attempting to understand how this flow takes place. Some students of politics, notably Karl Deutsch,[1] have argued that the key characteristic of a political system is its capability for handling and responding to the flow of messages it receives. Others would emphasise the argument that the health of democratic politics depends upon the rulers and the ruled not being too isolated from each other, lest confidence give way to apathy or alienation. It is thus important that the demands which we articulate be communicated in such a way that they are heard by those with responsibility for coping with them. The rulers should not merely rule, but should be seen to do so in a manner which accords with our expectations.

Political communication takes place at many levels. Richard Rose[2] suggests a distinction between horizontal communication, that between people at a similar level, whether élites or ordinary citizens, and vertical communication, that between people at different levels. Communication also takes place through a variety of means, which range from informal contacts between persons, to political parties and pressure groups which aggregate and crystallise political opinion, and to the communications media which are specifically dedicated to the business of transmitting and disseminating information to and from people at many levels.

When we study institutions whose business is communication, we do well to bear in mind that they, like the general networks of social communication to which they contribute, are only components, and not independent ones, of the wider social system. We have become so used to talking of 'media' as to be in danger of forgetting the literal implication of the term – that media operate to transmit messages which, for the most part, originate elsewhere in the social system. As Butler and Stokes remark about the press in Britain, 'readers are absorbing more than their editor's bias. A great deal of common information flows out to the British mass electorate through media which are heavily overlapping and which are describing political issues and events that they have seldom done anything to shape.'[3] This is a needed corrective to McLuhan's well-publicised thesis that the medium *is* the message. Nevertheless, it remains the case that an important consideration in any study of communications must be the extent to which the structure and needs of the medium as an institution determines the manner and content of its output. Even if the medium has done nothing to shape an issue or event, the 'news' which it gives the public is the end-product of a complex process of selection and shaping. To those involved, the criteria used in this process are no doubt so familiar as to be almost subconscious. But it is important that we try to determine what these are.

Few research operations investigating the character of particular media are likely to be so comprehensive that they can throw light on more than a few of the possible problems; while some, like that presented later in this study, are intentionally restricted in focus. Hence theories, models and concepts are essential, not only in pointing to the research problems which *are* tackled but also in relating these to the many which, for whatever reason, are not. Here, then, let us ask a series of questions. What functions do media perform in society, and in particular with respect to politics? What do people who use the media look for, and how are they affected by what they see? What are the rules of the game inside the medium as an organisation? What is 'news'? We shall deal with some of the issues raised by each of these in turn.

## THE SOCIAL FUNCTIONS OF MASS COMMUNICATION

Much of the theory that has been generated concerning the role of the media in society has tended to run along functionalist lines. A full-blown functionalist approach would operate upon the assumption that, since media exist, they must be making a certain contribution to the maintenance of the 'social system'. The theoretical debates surrounding functionalism in sociology have been complex and of wide significance for the ways in which we approach the interpretation of social phenomena. Most writers on the role of the media have, however, contented themselves with delineating their social functions in Western countries today. Lasswell,[4] writing in 1948, made an early proposal for functional analysis of mass communications, listing three basic elements which could be discerned in the activity of mass communication. These were (*a*) surveillance of the environment, that is to say the collection and distribution of information, or, in practical parlance, the gathering and presentation of 'news'; (*b*) the correlation of parts of society in responding to the environment, by which Lasswell meant that part of communication which is opinion forming, interpretative, editorial; (*c*) the transmission of the social heritage from one generation to the next, i.e. the induction of a new generation into the norms and values of its elders. Clearly this list could be added to. Charles R. Wright has suggested the addition of the function of entertainment, or amusement quite irrespective of any instrumental effects – and it is obvious that the media, including newspapers, are much looked to for this latter capacity. Merton and Lazarsfeld[5] put forward a further inventory of functions performed by the media vis-à-vis society. They argued that media perform an *ethicising* function – that is they uphold social norms and values by the publicity they give, both to them and to behaviour which deviates from them. They confer *status* – by automatically legitimising and hence enhancing the status of groups and individuals (and, it might be added, institutions and political procedures) to whom they give coverage. But their activities have the potentiality of what Merton and Lazarsfeld call a *narcotising* dysfunction. The oversupply of information, excitement, ideas, may create in people's minds an illusion of participation, a satisfaction with ersatz social action, while the community is starved of the real thing.

The idea of dysfunction, a central contribution to functional theory associated in the first instance with the name of Robert K. Merton, has been incorporated in a comprehensive scheme by Charles R. Wright.[6] Dysfunctions are observed consequences which lessen rather than contribute to the capacities for adaptation and adjustment, the self-maintenance capacities, of a given system. Wright brings together the contributions of Lasswell, Merton, Lazarsfeld and others in a general analytic scheme which defines the possible functions and dysfunctions of the several communication activities for different elements of the social structure, namely for 'society itself', for the individual, for sub-groups within the society such as, specifically, the political élite. As this set of formulations illuminates much research on mass communications it may be useful to cite it in full, though in a somewhat simplified form (see Table 2).

This approach, while of obvious attractiveness in the generation of questions leading to research and further theorising, has its weaknesses. It shares with the functional approach to society in general, a tendency to make too swift a leap from the fact that a phenomenon, the media, exists, to the conclusion that it must perform certain tasks 'for' society. Has society certain 'necessities' without which it cannot continue to exist in its present form? How socially 'necessary' is it that social norms and values be reinforced? Indeed, how certain

Table 2. *Functional analysis of mass communications*

| Communication activity | Functional and dysfunctional effects for: | | |
| --- | --- | --- | --- |
| | Society | Individual | Political élites |
| (a) Surveillance (news) — Functional | Instrumental – essential information for economy, and other institutions. | Instrumental – essential information. | Instrumental – information useful to maintenance of power. |
| | Warnings of dangers. Ethicising. | Warnings of dangers. Status conferment. | Detects and exposes deviant and subversive behaviour. Legitimises power, confers status. |
| Dysfunctional | Threatens stability; gives news of better possibilities. | Creates anxiety, privatisation, apathy. Narcotisation. | Threatens power, giving news of harsh realities, exposés, etc. |

Table 2—Continued

|  | | Society | Individual | Political élites |
|---|---|---|---|---|
| (b) Correlation (editorial work) | Functional | Aids mobilisation; impedes threats to social stability. Impedes panic. | Helps assimilation of news; impedes anxiety, privatisation, apathy. | Helps preserve power. |
|  | Dysfunctional | Increases social conformism; avoidance of criticism may impede social change. | Weakens critical faculties; increases passivity. | Increases responsibility. |
| (c) Cultural transmission | Functional | Increases social cohesion. Reduces anomie. Continues socialisation of adults. | Exposure to common norms aids integration. Reduces idiosyncrasy and anomie. | Extends power. Another agency for socialisation. |
|  | Dysfunctional | Augments mass society. | Depersonalises acts of socialisation. | |
| (d) Entertainment | Functional | Respite for the masses. | Respite. | Extends power over another area of life. |
|  | Dysfunctional | Diverts public from social action. | Increases passivity; lowers taste. | |

is it that we are not talking of the norms and values of particular segments of society? Are the media without choice in the matter of norms and values? Are not they themselves potentially important independently as value generators? It will hardly do to dismiss as dysfunctional a newspaper article, say, which adopts a stance highly critical of the powers that be. In short, we may impute social functions, manifest or latent, where none exist, and we may tend to view the media as reinforcing dominant groups and values in society, where there is more than a little difficulty in proving that this need *necessarily* be so. Of course, media managers might deliberately choose to do so, or do so unthinkingly by virtue of their own class or cultural predilections. But this falls short of what the concept 'function' is intended to convey. Let us finally acknowledge that the concept 'function' is used in a rather confusing variety of ways by the different writers concerned.

Nevertheless, and bearing these potential weaknesses in mind, much can be illuminated by the use of the perspectives this approach provides. If it is valid, for the purposes of analysis, to view society as a social system, we may, following Parsons, see 'the political' as a sub-system within it, or, as Easton has it, as a theoretically autonomous 'political system', in itself. Political scientists have used the idea in a variety of ways; for present purposes and for the purposes of the analysis offered in chapter 5, we may describe a political system as a set of structures and processes, the core of which is an authoritative centre of decision making. This is the focal point, for a given area and for given purposes, where the needs and problems of the area are perceived, interpreted, and ultimately acted upon. A series of stages leads up to the central decision-act, and a series of outcomes flows from it. The process involves the interplay of individuals and groups at a variety of levels, and in a variety of structures. It involves, too, their perceptions, dispositions and resources, the constitutional framework and the power relationships within which they operate. Since communication is an essential element in the system, the output of the media may be examined as it reflects the different elements and stages of the process, and as it makes its own independent contribution to the play of persons, pressures and policies. In so doing the media may help to enhance the authority of an élite, such as local government administrators, by giving legitimising comment and publicity to their activities. Or, media may contribute to the undermining of their power, by calling attention to facts incompatible with their claims to competence. Media may give valuable publicity to counter-groups, such as opposition parties or community organisations in conflict with city councils. For some people, however, they may act as a narcotic. If this could be substantiated, it would have an important bearing on the debate about popular participation in local affairs. Is it true that for many people a feeling of being kept informed is an adequate substitute for real involvement? This point can hardly be approached without some attention to the general problem of what makes for participation in politics, and here many variables as well as communication are clearly involved. But we may make a beginning by pursuing the emphasis on the functions which media use performs in the lives of users.

### WHY DO READERS READ?

Why do people read the local paper, and what do they get from it by way of rewards and gratifications? What effects does their exposure to it have on their perceptions and attitudes? The reader's use of his paper should form the context of any discussion of the importance of political news and information. Should it be discovered, for instance, that for the clientele of a particular paper, the imbibing of political news was only a minor by-product of reading a paper bought for quite other purposes, then the sheer volume of political coverage in that paper, or its nature, might not be particularly significant. Alternatively, many people may want to feel they are 'kept informed', in a general sense, but may be comparatively indifferent to the array of specific events they are informed *about*. In this case, it might well matter to them how much news of local council affairs was given in the local paper. But it might not matter particularly what that news consisted of, content being less important than the sheer volume of coverage in relation to other varieties of news.

British evidence on these matters is slight and, while the theory evolved for communications studies should be applicable in a variety of contexts, much of the literature on actual behaviour comes from the United States. We must, therefore, use it with some care. By comparison with Britain, the United States has no national press. Local and regional papers, carrying nationally syndicated material, serve the dual purpose of being local *and* national. They are often the 'voice' of a local community in the face of the larger United States which they monitor and interpret. They are thus, potentially, more weighty in relation to *their* local government. The weakness of parties as organisations, the prevalence of one-party areas, and the factionalism of dominant parties reinforces the power of the press. A newspaper staff know that they are key actors in the heavily personalised and factionalised politics of their city or locality. They can decisively influence 'new' candidates, especially in explicitly non-party situations such as exist in most of the smaller cities. Many American newspapers thus can be the only effective 'opposition' in the British sense. Their British counterparts operate in, for the most part, a context of well-organised parties who do not 'need' the newspaper to anything like the extent visible in the United States. Moreover, in Britain, the existence of a national press means that the local journalist is well aware that local leaders have access to alternative papers which are taken locally as widely as his own. He cannot aspire to the weight of his American opposite number, and his readers, conscious of their multifarious social and political loyalties and sources of information, might look askance if he tried to do so.

Undoubtedly, as Berelson[7] put it, 'different people read different parts of the newspaper for different reasons at different times', putting it to uses which do not always correspond with the newspaper's own avowed purposes. Working on the hypothesis that people are more conscious of what the paper means to them during a 'shock' period of deprivation rather than under normal conditions, Berelson studied the effects of a delivery men's strike which deprived New York of its papers for a fortnight in 1945. Berelson found that a general sense of being kept informed about the world, was what people most appreciated, though often this was not attached to items of specific 'serious' news content. He named five major values placed by his respondents on the paper. There was a core of people who genuinely wanted the world of public affairs brought to them. Some appreciated the personal social asset of appearing to be informed. Again, the papers provided a respite from personal care – hence the escape value of the 'human interest' story. They also provided an essential tool for daily living – with their lists of entertainments, goods for sale, commercial information, births, deaths and marriages. 'In short, there are many ways in which many people use the newspaper as a daily instrument or guide and it was missed accordingly.' Finally, they provided a characteristically twentieth-century form of social contact – 'they also supply guides to the prevailing morality, insight into private lives, as well as opportunity for vicarious participation in them, and indirect "personal" contact with distinguished people.' Berelson further suggested that, in so far as reading is in itself a pleasurable and socially approved activity in modern society, the newspaper was the most readily available and easily consumed source of these gratifications. In short, media use, in its various forms, takes place 'because it has met needs in the past, or . . . is being tried because it is expected to meet present needs'.[8]

Thus the significance of any particular aspect of newspaper coverage depends upon the place it has in the total pattern of the reader's responses to the newspaper. If it is only peripheral to the purposes for which he took up the paper, the effect which it has upon his perceptions will, to say the least, differ from its effect on someone consciously seeking out that type of news. Any real impact may well stem from the fact of his being taken unawares. What a reader 'gets' is determined by his background and his needs. He takes what he can use.

What do people in Britain look for in their papers? As in other aspects of newspaper reader research, there is information on the national press,[9] little or none on the local press, and to make inferences from the one to the other would be hazardous. Certain features, however, do stand out so strongly that they may hold true for both the local and national papers. Entertainment and relaxation appear to be more sought after the lower down the social scale the reader is placed. In the success of the *Daily Mirror*'s formula, a large part is played by the 'live letters' and the comic cartoons. But the dominant reason for buying the paper is for news – particularly perhaps for the details of news already known in outline from other sources rather than for 'up to the minute' news. People generally prefer reading 'news' to reading features, whether for information or entertainment. On the evidence of a Gallup survey in 1965, a front page lead story attracts to its subject twice the attention paid to the paper as a whole. On the other hand, though many see a paper daily, few read all of its news pages, and 'looking at the paper' may be no more than glancing at the headlines. A main headline, concerning a party conference, in the *Sunday Telegraph*, was subsequently followed up by only a third of the readers. Of news under another headline, on the same subject, only 40 per cent saw it, and less than 25 per cent actually read the item. In general, people like to be kept 'up to date' with the news but they have, on the whole, a relatively limited conception of what this entails. It appears to mean, for many British readers, what Berelson found for New Yorkers, namely the acquisition of a general, unspecific sense of being abreast of affairs rather than a demand for specific information on specific topics. R. V. Clements' survey of Bristol businessmen[10] revealed that they relied a good deal on the local paper to find out 'what's going on', and high in their list of reasons for giving it attention was the news it gave of business and social activities in the city. They liked to read of their friends' activities. Lord Thomson asserts that much of the appeal of local papers is that 'people like to see local names, local streets'. There is clearly much that is valued in the regular news of births, deaths and marriages, which alone ensure the mention of hundreds, if not thousands, of families in the

paper each year. Add to this classified advertisements, useful information such as matters concerning roadworks etc. Politics, as such, is
of interest largely as a branch of general news – and some 'political'
news is simply not popular at all. Doubt may be expressed as to
how much 'political' news is actually read at all or, if read,
assimilated.

## THE EFFECTS OF COMMUNICATION

What impact does newspaper reading have upon the attitudes of the
reader? This is a complex issue. We should note at once that the
impact of one medium will have other media as part of its context.
People who read the local press may also be listeners to the radio,
watchers of television and readers of books. They are almost
certainly also readers of national newspapers. Research on the effect
of television[11] may give guidelines suggestive of the impact of other
media. This research suggests that media impact reaches maximal
levels where there is a cumulative barrage of broadly identical news
and values over a period; where what is presented has links with the
receptor's own immediate needs and interests; where attachment to
the medium is uncritical and other sources of stimulus are un-
important; where the immediate environment of the individual does
not already supply him with a set of values on which to base a
critical stance; and where the individual is psychologically ready to
learn about certain issues. Butler and Stokes, while accepting the
broad thesis that the better informed person is likely to be less
impressionable in that any new information has to find its way into
'a complex circuitry' of previously acquired 'connections', nevertheless argue that there can be circumstances in which the elector with
*greater* exposure is the likelier to change his views on receipt of
important new information. Between 1964 and 1966 it was those
most exposed to political communication who most altered their
views on the Common Market. Butler and Stokes' general conclusion is that papers do have an impact on reader opinion – they help
to 'magnetise' the party they support for those readers already disposed to support it (conversely they helped to spread disenchantment
among the Conservatives during 1963), but that in doing so they
are only one element among many in the creation of opinion.[12]

Without research well beyond the scope of the present investigation
we cannot tell what the local newspapers' performance on these

criteria might be. But with regard to local politics it is in the position of having a virtual monopoly in the supply of information. It fulfils needs of a certain sort, which are provided, for those who require them, by no rival. Attachment to the medium and the absence of alternative institutions of communication as far as local government is concerned may also be important. On the other hand, we may reiterate the argument that much that is in the paper is unread or quickly forgotten unless the individual reader can find a place for it in his personal frame of reference, or can find escape/gratification in it. We may suggest further that a considerable portion of political coverage, and perhaps particularly that concerning British local government as at present administered, may fall into this category. The local government system itself may not be entirely at fault. If people view it with apathy, it may be that they have little choice because the press offers them news of it which, by its nature and presentation, keeps them ignorant and gives local government a duller image than need be. Hence the importance of a study of what is offered and why. Further, since local government exists to administer a range of services, we may suggest that while it may be the case that people in *general* are bewildered as to what local government does, they might be better seen not 'in general' at all but as a set of specific consumers of specific services, which, severally, do relate very much to their personal frames of reference, though what concerns one man may not concern another. Again, whatever may be case of the majority, some, the political activists, are *very* interested in what is presented as news, and these people, inevitably, tend to include many of the influentials. *What* they read is important.

## THE NEWSPAPER AS AN ORGANISATION

The newspaper's business, said the great Delane, is 'to obtain the earliest and most correct intelligence of the events of the time and instantly, by disclosing them, to make them the common property of mankind'.[13] True, no doubt, but not so simple. The news that appears upon the page is the end-product of a complex process. The 'event' has to take place in a 'reportable' fashion. If it does not, someone may have to 'shape' it into a reportable form. Someone has to decide that it is an 'event' at all. And the form of treatment it gets may be dictated by forces and needs internal to the newspaper as an organisation which may have little or nothing to do with the 'event' itself. What forces, then, can we observe as acting between 'events' and what appears in print?

There has been comparatively little research on media organisations as such. Newspapers, as we noted earlier, must make profits; but they are also very much in the public eye, and too ruthless a pursuit of economic ends may mean conflict with the need for prestige and respect in the community. Journalists must give their public what they like to read; but they also feel it a public duty to print certain types of news which many readers may find dull. The way these values are balanced may vary a great deal from one newspaper to another. In the same way there is great scope for variation in the actual internal structure of newspaper organisation. This was revealed very clearly by the Economist Intelligence Unit's Report (1966)[14] on the national newspaper industry. 'Although the status of the editorial function is very high in all newspapers', the report comments, 'its powers vary from organisation to organisation.' In several, the editor's powers were paramount and the editor had almost unlimited freedom of action; but in others there appeared a trend towards more rigorous control over editorial departments. The authors of the report were surprised at the width of variations even between broadly similar publications – the *Daily Express*, they found, had at that time 60 per cent more reporters than the *Daily Mail*.

The communicator, then, is embedded in a work situation which needs to be understood as an integral part of any study of how and what he communicates. He has to be seen in terms of the authority and sanctions of his employers, the newspaper's policy, the professional ethics of his colleagues, and the informal structures which have been built up by these, in combination, over time. A newspaper staff is a micro-social system in itself. It is more, or less, conducive to the realisation of its members' aims. It is more, or less, well integrated, managed with greater or less efficiency. It is more, or less, well adjusted to its environment. Journalists, like people in any other occupation, tend to work to guidelines evolved by in-groups of their colleagues. News selection is governed by rules of established practice which, as elsewhere, are loaded with the conventional wisdom of the trade. Breed[15] describes how the new 'staffer' was socialised, in the American newspaper, to conform to the policy norms of the paper rather than his own personal beliefs; the atmosphere of the office clearly discouraged journalists from taking an interest in 'serious' affairs. In short, 'the fate of the local news story is not determined by the needs of the audience or even by the values of the symbols it contains. The news story is controlled by the bureaucratic structure of which the communicator is a member.'

Key members of this structure have been termed 'gatekeepers'. Kurt Lewin observed that information does not flow by its own impetus but enters channels guarded at several points by people who decide whether or not an item will be transmitted further, or in the same form. We may apply this to any person in a newspaper office who makes news choices. The analytic task is to discern who is in that position and what criteria he adopts in his choices. At worst, it is he who passes on to the community only those facts and events he believes they should know about. His choices will be determined by his own personal values and background and also by his picture of the audience to whom his work is ultimately addressed. So in any study we will want to know, not only who the gatekeepers are, but also what their values, attitudes and expectations are, what their past experiences have been, and how they relate to the community they are operating in. Does a journalist with a purely 'local' past and projected future judge 'news' by a different set of criteria than one with a more cosmopolitan background whose relationship to his present job and town is more instrumental?

The processes by which news is gathered and produced may be represented in Figure 1:

Raw news—→News copy—→News processors—→Completed product

*Figure 1*[16]

The actions may be virtually concertinaed into one movement; gathering and processing may also be in the hands of the same person or persons. And the smaller the organisation, the more one would expect this to be the case. Yet in all but the smallest newspaper there will be a degree of differentiation more or less along the lines indicated. Hence, between the taking place of an 'event', and the reception by the reader of an account of it, a considerable modification and shaping has taken place. In practice, however, much local paper activity consists less in 'processing' news than in sifting and selecting items whose 'form' is largely already 'given' in the shape of speeches, annual reports of council officials, accounts of committee and council proceedings, etc. A study of factors limiting the 'community surveillance effort' of 18 American daily newspapers concluded that the amount of wire news from the press agencies was the key factor determining coverage and that it may be meaningless to speak of the local press in the United States as carrying out much of a uniquely *local* surveillance role outside of the traditional town hall and courthouse 'beats'. The mix of factors limiting press freedom in news selection was represented diagrammatically as in

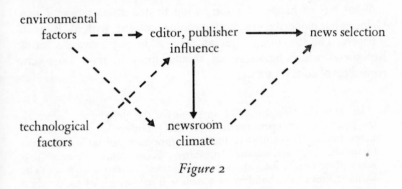

*Figure 2*

Figure 2[17] with the stronger lines representing direct, and the broken indirect or weaker influence.

WHAT IS NEWS?

We are left with the question, what is news? That is to say, which events and which aspects of those events, are likely to become raw material for processing into news? As Walter Lippman noted many years ago, newspapers do not keep an eye on all mankind – they watch, or employ people to watch, the comparatively small number of places where it is made known where and when anyone departs from ordinary paths. Something definite must occur that has an unmistakable form. News, he said, has to await an overt act, because the paper is constrained by 'the economy of noting only the stereo-typed phase of a situation, the difficulty of finding journalists who can see what they've not learned to see . . . the economic necessity of interesting the reader quickly, the economic risk of not interesting him at all'.[18] Hence a strike is news but the conditions leading to a strike are not, unless some board of investigation has produced a sensational report. In general, investigation of the latent and the un-overt is beyond the resources of most newspapers. 'A great deal, I think myself the crucial part, of what looks to the worker and reformer as a deliberate misrepresentation on the part of newspapers, is the direct outcome of a practical difficulty of making distant facts interesting.' Here, Lippman might well be summarising the problems facing local government reportage. In his terms, much of the output of local government is, from the reportage point of view, unnewsworthy.

What has to happen for something to qualify as news? Johan Galtung has pioneered exploration of this problem; with M. Ruge in a paper, 'The structure of foreign news',[19] he put forward a set of hypotheses which he suggested should apply in most situations, regardless of cultural setting.

1. The more the 'frequency' of an event fits the 'frequency' on which the news medium operates, the more is it probable that it will become news, taking 'frequency' to mean the time-span needed for an event to unfold itself and acquire 'meaning'. For instance, an event that takes place over a long time-span is difficult to record as news. The inauguration of the building of a dam will be noticed, its construction much less so. A death on the roads is news, a death in battle is not, for it is the battle itself which is news.
2. An event must overcome a threshold before it is considered newsworthy at all.
3. Convention will dictate which event conveys a clear meaning and which does not. An event which has a clear interpretation, free from ambiguities in meaning, is preferable to one which is ambiguous in its message.
4. There must be a degree of ethnocentrism in the event, i.e. it must have some meaning for the receptor (this is especially important in the case of foreign news).
5. News fits mental-pre-images, that is, a person predicts that something will happen, is mentally tuned to it happening, and thus when an event that fits the pre-image takes place, it is interpreted in that light.
6. But, given this framework, it is the ad hoc, the rare, that will receive attention rather than the regular, the repetitive, the institutionalised.
7. Once an event has hit the headlines and become 'news', an area of 'news' has been opened up and it will continue to be defined as 'news', partly through inertia, partly to justify the original selection of the event as 'news'. Further, once something is defined as news that which has made it newsworthy is likely to be accentuated.
8. The need to present news as a balanced whole means that the thres-

holds vary from item to item, and from time to time, depending upon the totality of raw news coming in to the newspaper office.

Galtung and Ruge conclude that, on this basis, it is possible to set up a list of newsworthiness criteria, varying with the aims and cultural setting of the news medium. The more events satisfy the criteria, the more likely it is that they will be registered as news. Negative news, i.e. bad news, fits the frequency criterion better than positive, because the negative consists often of breaks of routine and of norms such as disasters, strikes, accidents. It is more likely to fit the unexpectedness criterion. In the West there is a tendency for news to be personalised and about élite people, for similar reasons.

If these hypotheses are correct, certain consequences flow from them which, valid for all newspapers, are particularly problematic for the local newspaper reporting local politics. The normal is not news. Progress can pass unreported. So can the slow unfolding of municipal programmes, because their frequency fits ill with that on which the press operates. In the case of planning and redevelopment, the normal functioning of well oiled and satisfactory procedures can, at best, be accorded an account of the intention, beginning, and conclusion stages of a scheme, with perhaps the occasional interim report or photograph. This for something that may shape the face and future of an area in a substantial way. One single complaint by the residents affected, or by traders losing business as a result of population change may receive, overall, as much treatment. Planning officials and committees might well feel aggrieved. The *ad hoc*, the rare, the unexpected, in local political life, is likely to be fairly trivial or hard to come by, compared with the national or international scene. The tendency to process news by presenting it in terms of élite figures is difficult, if not impossible, in relation to local political personages. This may be precluded by the lack of social distance between the personages, the reporters, and their public. Moreover, local notables may have the sanction to hand of their own control over the flow of raw news. Finally, however, we must draw attention to the pre-image of local government as 'dull' which, it may be argued, inhibits reporters from experimenting with ways of presenting it in a more lively fashion. (The treatment of news in the Soviet Union presents a cautionary contrast for those disposed to charge Western news media with triviality. There, only 'significant' events are reported, crime, accidents and 'human interest' being largely neglected. Since the general trend, particularly economic, is important, topicality is not a prime issue. Hence the jocular charge that there is no 'news' in Pravda.)

Local government in Britain lends itself to the dramatic only on rare, and these perhaps misleading, occasions. What the newspaper reader learns of it must largely be confined to glimpses of a governmental machine ticking over in a state of steady, on-going performance, busying itself with administration but, much of the time, lacking the high drama and the concern with great issues that often appear to suffuse the Westminster scene. In neither case, local nor central, may the popular image of government be a true one. British local government has a larger sphere of competence than that which is commonly attributed to it, but nevertheless its activities are largely the local working out of trends and policies determined nationally. The bulk of the most newsworthy 'big' local political events are of two types, both occurring comparatively infrequently. First, there is the event of the taking of a decision of community-wide significance which, unlike most such decisions, lies within the local authority's competence: on comprehensive schools, for example, or on town-centre redevelopment. Secondly, there is the occasional instance of 'breakdown' in a part of the system, such as a bus strike.

If it is a characteristic of media to concentrate on such atypical events, the student of the media must himself beware of concentrating on a part only of the surveillance which is offered. He, too, may be guilty of coming to a distorting conclusion. The recent study by members of the Leicester University Centre for Mass Communications Research, of the demonstration in Grosvenor Square on 27 October 1968[20] has been criticised for its emphasis on the coverage of the 'event itself', on the day itself, divorced from consideration of the general context of media coverage of events of that type, and including the coverage given in the weeks preceding the event. 'By confining their examination of television news to the day of the demonstration', says one critic, the Leicester team limited the validity of their findings. 'There was no attempt to look at the overall coverage of the demonstration before October 27th, nor to discover what steps the broadcasting authorities took to balance their coverage.'[21] This specific controversy is out of place here; but we can at least give the fullest possible picture by applying our analysis not merely to what constitutes news in the sense of the front page, the 'event', but also to all coverage in the sense that that term includes the features on the inside pages; and by operating within a time span so broad that the idiosyncrasies caused by specific and perhaps non-recurring events can be smoothed down to take their place in an overall picture.

What is needed is a formula for content analysis which, however crudely, aims at placing the parts in a whole. The method of examining the content of newspaper coverage which is discussed and utilised in chapter 5 is an attempt to do so. In it some of the main components of the political system concept are used to analyse all the coverage of the local political scene in six papers over an eight-year period.

# 4

## Merseyside in the 1960s

An examination of any city will reveal features which are unique to it and ones which it has in common with others of its time and type. Merseyside in the 1960s reflected Britain in the 1960s, but did so in ways peculiar to itself. The trend of population movement continued outwards from inner to fringe areas. Car ownership increased. Large areas of poor housing remained, despite strenuous efforts to attack the problem. City planning as an organised enterprise got firmly under way. The relationship between demands and resources in the provision of public services was, and continues to be, one of the greatest of local political problems – most visibly in the area of public transport. The industrial base of the conurbation was diversified, though results were not entirely satisfactory since the area's tradition of industrial conflict was, to some extent, continued in the new settings.

But what is Merseyside? Definitions of an urban area will inevitably vary according to the purposes for which definition is needed. At one extreme, Merseyside is a city region stretching from the Ribble to north-eastern Wales. It stretches less deeply east into Lancashire, where before long the countervailing influence of Manchester is felt. Within this wide area commuting into the inner area takes place, and there is economic and social dependence on the services provided by the core. For instance, three large Liverpool stores deliver goods by van weekly to customers as far north as Blackpool and as far west as Conway. Merseyside may also be defined simply as the continuous built-up area, the conurbation. The Redcliffe–Maud definition was a compromise between this and a full city region. Our principal concern, however, is with an area yet smaller – the four inner county boroughs of Liverpool, Bootle, Birkenhead and Wallasey. Arbitrary though their boundaries may be, these four boroughs shared a common local government status, being the four single-tier authorities in the conurbation. These are, of course, to a greater or lesser extent, interdependent both with each other and with the wider city region.

Newspapers in their coverage and areas of circulation reflect this.

The dailies circulate within the entire city region and beyond, and the weeklies produced in the smaller county boroughs do not cease to circulate once the borough boundary is crossed. Local journalists, then, must operate with a sense of both a *local* society and polity, a local economy *and* some notions of region and/or conurbation. What kind of area are journalists likely to have been aware of and what are the differences between the component parts?

In terms of aggregate population the trends of the 1960s vary as definitions of the conurbation and its hinterland vary.[1] If we take one of the fairly wide definitions, the Redcliffe–Maud one, we include an area from Southport in the north, through St Helens in the east to below Chester in the south. This area recorded a net population increase of 5 per cent in the 1950s and some 3 per cent in the early 1960s. If we take a more restricted definition – say that of the 1951 census – we add to the four inmost boroughs the local authorities of Wirral, Hoylake, Ellesmere Port, Neston, Bebington in Cheshire, and Crosby, Huyton-with-Roby and Litherland in Lancashire. This area barely increased its population in the 1950s and in the 1960s began to record a net loss as the natural increase lessened and failed to match the rate of outward migration.[2]

The areas of heaviest outward migration were precisely the areas of our principal concern, namely the four boroughs at the heart of the conurbation. Their combined populations stood at 1,107,000 in 1951, made up as follows: Liverpool 790,000; Birkenhead 142,000; Wallasey 101,000; Bootle 74,000. They recorded a net loss of population of 3 per cent in the 1950s and a further 6 per cent loss between 1961 and 1966. In the 1950s the source of this loss was the city of Liverpool – Bootle gaining 12 per cent, Wallasey 2 per cent and Birkenhead standing still. Between 1961 and 1966, however, all four recorded net losses, the figures being: Liverpool – down 7 per cent to 691,000; Bootle – down 6 per cent to 78,000; Birkenhead – down 2 per cent to 139,000; and Wallasey – down 3 per cent to 100,000. The causes of this loss are complex, though it can be said that chief among them were outward migration and falling birth rates after 1961.[3]

Comparison between the situation in the four boroughs serves as some guide to their characters. Liverpool and Birkenhead present very similar class profiles with the skilled working class groups comprising nearly a half of the whole population and semi- and unskilled just over a third. Wallasey and Bootle stand in very clear contrast. In Bootle, the middle class is very thin on the ground and the semi- and unskilled residents are almost as large a group as the skilled. Bootle, of course, is a near one-class town. Wallasey has – in contrast – a high proportion of middle class residents and a low proportion, about a quarter, are semi- and unskilled residents.

In terms of class structure the changes over a decade and a half were relatively slight. All four boroughs showed a decline in the skilled working class groups and, save for Liverpool, all record an increase in the semi- and unskilled working class population. Liverpool and Bootle show an increase in Classes I and II while both Wirral boroughs revealed a decline in the relative size of their resident middle class population.

The class structure gives a clue to the various political pre-occupations of the boroughs, and the age structure of their populations provides more. All four boroughs rank above the England and Wales figure of 22·9 per cent for the 0–14 age group, startlingly so in the case of Bootle with 30·1 per cent. Only Wallasey at 13·5 per cent exceeds the England and Wales figure of 12·4 per cent for the retired 65 + age group – Bootle again being noticeably deviant at 8·5 per cent. All four boroughs, comparing the 1952 and 1966 figures, shared in the steady increase in the proportion of retired people. The size of the young and increase in the older age groups would lead one to hypothesise a marked sensitivity to education and welfare services of all kinds.

An important factor in such sensitivity would be the various questions involved in the housing situation. The figures for one measure of housing need, namely density of population, are reveal-ing. In 1961 the density of population per acre was as follows – Bootle 27·1 persons, Liverpool 26·8, Birkenhead 16·5 and Wallasey 17·5. Nearly 12 per cent of persons in Liverpool were living at a density greater than one and a half per room, while in eight of the city's forty wards over 20 per cent were doing so. By 1966 the proportion for the city as a whole had been reduced to 5 per cent, while that in Vauxhall ward, the most dense in 1961, had been reduced from 36 per cent to 17 per cent. The change that this represents in the situation since 1951 – in aggregate terms – is dramatic for all the boroughs, with the rate of improvement much increased in the 1960s. Yet – Wallasey apart – the aggregate picture is still fairly striking. Measured by this index, Liverpool, Bootle and

Birkenhead are worse off, not just by the standard of England and Wales, but also by that of the Northwest, and this by a substantial margin in the case of Bootle and Liverpool.[4] In 1961 over 50 per cent of dwellings in the four boroughs had been built before 1914, significantly, again, above the mean figure for England and Wales. Housing then, in the 1960s, would have been likely to be a first class social and political problem.

These social changes and attendant problems were part product and part cause of economic changes which have occurred since the heyday of the port of Liverpool came to an end after 1918. Merseyside, after all, while not Jarrow, was also synonymous with desperate unemployment in the 1930s, caused by its heavy dependence on the docks, shipbuilding and ship-repairing industries. Merseyside had 28 per cent unemployed in 1932, while for most of the period since the war the rate has been over twice the national average. Hence, the 1950s and 1960s were marked by attempts to diversify and modernise local industry. The opening of the Ford plant at Halewood in 1962 was a nationally recognised symbol of an area seeking not only to change its image but its economic base.

The port of Liverpool remained, nevertheless, the country's second port and a large local employer. The Census category of Transport and Communications accounted for 88,800, 12·8 per cent of all Merseyside jobs in the early 1960s as against 6 per cent for Britain as a whole. This reflected the importance of the port. Figures vary with definitions as to how many jobs the docks themselves are responsible for. However, in 1966, a reasonable estimate would be that the docks in Liverpool provided 11,500 jobs, those in Bootle 3,500 jobs and those in the Wallasey–Birkenhead complex some 3,000 jobs. The actual dock labour force was somewhat smaller than this and during the 1960s gradually shrank in size, especially in the older Liverpool sector.

Bootle still shows heavy male dependence on the Mersey docks and dock-based employment. From cargo handling, storage and shipping and allied occupations, something like 28–30 per cent of the male workforce derives its income directly. When women workers are counted, dock-based employment accounts for even more of Bootle's workforce.[5] Women outnumber men by some 2:1 in clerical and sales jobs and, generally, in the service sector. The large expansion of employment in this sector in Bootle has been its success story of the 1960s. What Halewood and Ford symbolised for

Liverpool, the winning of the Post Office Giro complex symbolised for Bootle in 1966 – not only acknowledgment of economic necessity, but also recognition of the town's entrepreneurial skills. And there were other successes too, in attracting office employment by nationally known concerns such as the Midland Bank. Given the penetration of the administrative side of the dock industry by women, in addition to their dominance in clerical and sales service jobs, women form a large and growing sector of the Bootle workforce and a sizeable contribution to the local economy. The success of Bootle in building this sector in the 1960s is very significant for the town.

Bootle's portion of the Mersey docks retained its viability and prosperity. Confidence in it was reinforced by the commencement of building on a great new dock complex at Seaforth, just north of the town. On the other hand, the prospect of containerisation of freight, though guaranteeing continued prosperity of trade, did not seem to guarantee employment. Estimates vary considerably as to the probable impact of containerisation on Merseyside dock employment. By 1991 reductions in the labour force from the 1961 figure have been estimated at as much as 90 per cent or as little as 25 per cent, depending on the thoroughness of the container revolution. Most of the loss would be in the older dock areas of Liverpool rather than further north along the Mersey or on the Cheshire side. Most of it lies in the future. But in the 1960s, for those involved, it could not but be a source of apprehension. Hence all the boroughs, but particularly Bootle and Liverpool, had cause to temper their preoccupation with dock employment with an urge to reduce their dependence upon it.

By contrast with Bootle, the preponderance in Wallesey[6] is very clearly white collar – something over 40 per cent of male workers and over 60 per cent of the women workers being in clerical, sales, managerial and professional, technical categories. Yet the docks are also important in employment, some 10 per cent of the workforce being engaged in the handling, moving and storing of cargoes and servicing of shipping generally. Wallasey too, has sought to diversify its local economy, and the size of its engineering and allied trades sector is some evidence of this. But Wallasey is primarily a residential area for thousands of managerial and clerical workers who work either in the Wirral or commute to Liverpool. The community is, naturally, much concerned with easy and inexpensive commutation.

Birkenhead exhibits a somewhat more evenly balanced distribution of occupation. The shipbuilding and ship-repairing concern of Cammell Lairds employs some 10 per cent of male workers. So, too, do the docks and allied occupations. Upwards of 25 per cent of men and over 50 per cent of women workers are clerical, sales, managerial, technical and professional workers.[7] As in Wallasey, many of them are commuters to Liverpool. Its commuter preoccupation is equalled by its concern for the future of shipbuilding and of the docks – both of which for some years have given cause for anxiety.

Liverpool is currently the most balanced of all four boroughs in respect of occupational structure, having overcome a great dependence on the Port. Some 10 per cent of male workers are still employed at the docks, while 22 per cent of the men and 50 per cent of women workers are in clerical, sales, professional and technical jobs. In addition to these, however, the proportion of workers in engineering, electronics and food processing – over 20 per cent – is testimony to the successful entry of the city into car assembly, light engineering and manufacturing in general.[8] Liverpool is concerned with continuing diversification and retaining its position as the economic focus of a wide hinterland.

The incidence of car-ownership on Merseyside by 1966 is a measure of a new kind of preoccupation and new demands on local authority responsibility. The 1962 Merseyside Traffic Survey revealed that in the 1950s car ownership in Liverpool increased at 20 per cent per annum, while in Birkenhead the figure was 15 per cent. By 1966, 34 per cent of house holders on Merseyside had one or more cars. This compared with 46 per cent for England generally and 36 per cent for the neighbouring greater Manchester area.[9] Over the conurbation as a whole, of course, car-ownership is much denser in the suburbs on the Wirral and outer north Merseyside than in the inner areas of the four central boroughs. The growth and diversification of the local economy and the outward spread of residential areas has resulted in a large commuting workforce. Between 1951 and 1966, while in the West Midlands the numbers travelling to work increased by 97 per cent, on Merseyside this figure was 138 per cent, which represented more than double the previous total.

One result of this was the overloading of the Mersey tunnel between Liverpool and Birkenhead. In the early 1960s the movement towards the building of a second tunnel got under way and agreement to build it between Liverpool and Wallasey was reached. It was opened in 1971.

Merseyside in general, then, had become more prosperous. It had not, however, done exceptionally well compared to, say, the West Midlands. And within the conurbation the four boroughs had done less well again. All four had engaged in redevelopment, overspill and rehousing yet, by the late 1960s, there remained sizeable pockets of citizens living in considerable poverty and considerably larger numbers of lower income families and the old for whom 'the affluent society' was a description of other people's lives.

The need to tackle the physical, social and environmental problems of the city in a new way was recognised in Liverpool by the creation, in the early 1960s, of a City Planning Department, which rapidly grew both in size and prestige. None of the other boroughs did this, leaving planning as part of the functions of the borough engineer.

Merseyside is popularly considered to have a distinctive political flavour due to heavy immigration from Ireland, and this was certainly true in the past. At the high point of Irish immigration, in the 1850s, half the migrants into Liverpool were Irish and in 1861 one in four of the city's population had been born in Ireland.[10] Not all of them stayed in the area, but those who did were reinforced by a steady trickle of further immigrants continuing until the early years of the twentieth century. The city had its own Irish Nationalist party, with one M.P., while in response the Conservative party was closely associated with Orangeism. Between the wars the Labour party took over the allegiance and participation of the bulk of the former Irish party's supporters, and this was a crucial step in the 'normalisation' of Liverpool city politics. A small Protestant party, holding two wards with Conservative support, remained. By the 1960s Merseyside politics was little more affected by the politics of religious cleavage than any other area in England. In the 1961 census only 2·3 per cent of the population of the four county boroughs had been born in Ireland. The descendants of the former Irish immigrants were almost all second, third or fourth generation Merseysiders. The Conservative party continued to enjoy rather more support than the average for areas with comparable social composition, while the Labour party was considered by some observers to have inherited a structure slightly more reminiscent of the ethnic politics of American cities than is general in Britain.[11] The number of Roman Catholics in Merseyside was notably greater than the national average, particularly in working class districts such as north Liverpool and Bootle, and this was a factor making for greater political sensitivity in some fields, notably education. In general, however, in the 1960s, this was the sum total of the residue from the area's once stormy political past. Most of the time its effect on politics was scarcely discernible.

Party fortunes in the four boroughs in the 1960s followed the general pattern of English local elections. The tide flowed strongly with the Labour party during the first half of the decade, turned in 1964–5, and then flowed even more strongly with the Conservatives, who were at the end of the decade in firm control of most of English local government. 1964 was the year of Labour's greatest predominance over Conservative. But of course in each borough the movement took place within parameters distinctive to itself. Labour never gained control in Wallasey, while they never lost it in Birkenhead, the only borough of the four to remain in the control of the same party throughout the decade. By 1969 Labour was in control of the town only by virtue of almost total control of the aldermanic bench, and it was to lose this control in 1970. In Wallasey the parties were evenly balanced for the first half of the period, with the Liberals holding the balance. In 1966 the Conservatives established overall control. Liverpool was in Labour control from 1963, and, with Bootle, switched from Labour to Conservative in 1967. Table 3 shows the position (councillors and aldermen) at the beginning, middle and end of the period under review.

Table 3. *Party strengths on councils (councillors and aldermen) 1962–69*

| | 1962 | '66 | '69 | 1962 | '66 | '69 |
|---|---|---|---|---|---|---|
| | | Liverpool | | | Bootle | |
| Conservative | 81 | 66 | 110 | 16 | 18 | 40 |
| Labour | 73 | 86 | 41 | 40 | 38 | 14 |
| Liberal | 2 | 2 | 3 | | | |
| Protestant | 4 | 5 | 6 | | | |
| Others | 0 | 0 | 0 | | | |
| | | Birkenhead | | | Wallasey | |
| Conservative | 24 | 19 | 27 | 25 | 33 | 43 |
| Labour | 38 | 43 | 34 | 24 | 22 | 12 |
| Liberal | 2 | 2 | 2 | 12 | 4 | 7 |
| Protestant | | | | | | |
| Others | | | 1 | 3 | 5 | 2 |

It will be noticed that the relatively homogeneous working class nature of Bootle did not prevent it from sustaining a Conservative party strong enough to win as great a majority over Labour in the council in 1969 as Labour had over Conservative eight years earlier. With only seven wards, each with double representation, a sweeping change of hands was more possible than elsewhere. Wallasey, though the most middle class of the boroughs, was nonetheless capable of denying the Conservatives' control, if not of giving it to another party. It had the highest electoral turnout, Liverpool having the lowest.

Failure to reform the ward boundaries was a source of grievance in two of the boroughs, and in Birkenhead this was an important factor in explaining the persistence of the Labour party in control. In the 1960s two wards, both Conservative in disposition, contained 30 per cent of the boroughs' population, but enjoyed only 12½ per cent of the representation on the council. By contrast a similar population in eight inner wards of the town, Labour in disposition, enjoyed 50 per cent of the representation. A similar situation obtained in Wallasey, where the two wards of the town's recently developed west end had 25 per cent of the population with 12½ per cent of the representation. Here, however, the implications for party control were fairly slight.

The meaning of party control for local authorities is a complex one. Research suggests that a change of control would not necessarily lead to a specific set of policy outcomes.[12] Even in the case of comprehensive education there were, in the 1960s, Labour controlled boroughs sluggish in introducing it, Conservative ones efficient in doing so. Broadly speaking, however, the tendency is for Labour control to mean higher spending, particularly on the bigger services like education and housing. Conservatives, while in general tending to rein in expenditure, may well spend more on general amenities, welfare services and the police. In general, too, Labour control tends to mean tighter party dominance over local authority affairs, with much less business expedited in full council, and a tendency not to give officials their head, except when in pursuance of programmes with which the party is in accord.[13] To the extent that this is the case, it would have implications for public knowledge of council affairs, which, *prima facie*, should be easier to obtain under a Conservative than a Labour council, other things being equal.

To all generalisations such as these there are bound to be exceptions, and Birkenhead was one such. Controlled by Labour since 1949, the council has been tightly controlled and officials relatively subordinated to party dominance. Yet this has been accompanied by a very low rate policy both by the standards of the region and by those of County Boroughs of similar composition. Expenditure on services has been equally low and many of these in consequence have been underdeveloped.[14]

Finally, how was the conurbation served by the local press? Chiefly, by the *Liverpool Daily Post* and the *Liverpool Echo*. These are owned by the Liverpool Daily Post and Echo Ltd, and are produced from the same office. There is thus a degree of common hierarchy and a policy of interchangeability of staff. The *Wallasey News* and the *Birkenhead News* form, with four (formerly three) other Wirral papers, a group known as West Cheshire Newspapers Ltd, which had in 1970 a combined circulation of 91,865. The *Bootle Times Herald* was formed after the amalgamation in 1965 of the two papers whose names are reflected in the title, the former of which had been acquired by the Liverpool Daily Post and Echo Ltd two and a half years earlier. One of the Southport Visiter (sic) group of newspapers, the *Bootle Times Herald*, is in association with other papers circulating in the northern suburbs of Merseyside. Both these groups in turn are subsidiaries of the main company, the Daily Post and Echo Ltd, the late Sir Alick Jeans having been a director of all three.

The only newspaper which is wholly independent of this nexus is the *Liverpool Weekly News*, which originally started life in 1885 as the *Garston and Woolton Weekly News*, and which still circulates in and concentrates its coverage on the southern sections of the city. It is now associated with two other newspapers in the Weekly News Group, whose head office is in Widnes.

The Audit Bureau of Circulations gave the following circulation figures at the end of the 1960s.[15]

| | |
|---|---|
| *Liverpool Daily Post* | 96,396 |
| *Liverpool Echo* | 389,367 |
| *Liverpool Weekly News* | 43,211 |
| *Wallasey News* | 20,788 |
| *Birkenhead News* (*Wed.*) | 16,289 |
| *Birkenhead News* (*Fri.*) | 41,562 |
| *Bootle Times Herald* | 13,403 |

It would be hazardous, given the differences in circulation areas, to draw conclusions from these figures, except to comment on the sheer weight in terms of circulation of the *Liverpool Echo*, which daily sells over three times the number of copies sold by all the weekly papers combined. At the same time it, with the *Daily Post*, circulates not only in the three smaller boroughs but well beyond Merseyside, penetrating far into North Wales.

Some idea of the interpenetration of the staffs of these groups with the *Post* and the *Echo*, and the hierarchical values involved may be gained by noting some changes which took place in 1969. The managing editor of West Cheshire Newspapers moved to the *Liverpool Echo* as Assistant Editor (Sport). This was presumably a promotion. The new managing editor of West Cheshire Newspapers had been the *Post*'s Night News Editor and previously the *Post* and the *Echo*'s Birkenhead reporter.

Towards the end of the period, in 1967, the papers were joined by Radio Merseyside, one of the first of the B.B.C.'s new local radio stations. Where other cities, such as Manchester, had doubts about local radio and held back from it, Liverpool's self-image as a city with panache impelled it into this new venture in local communication. For the first two years of its existence, however, it was fed with news by the *Post* and the *Echo* office. As it could only be heard on V.H.F. transmitters its potential audience was limited. While acknowledging that it produced some very worthwhile political programmes, we have not included it in this study except for survey responses reported in chapter 8.

This, then, was the social and economic setting in which local government and politics operated in the 1960s, and these were the papers with the responsibility for covering the scene. Local politics, while reflecting issues and problems common to cities throughout the nation, are moulded into specific patterns by local social needs and resources and the political dispositions that emerge from particular social compositions. We would, therefore, expect there to be differences of political preoccupation and differences of style in dealing with problems from town to town. One American study, Williams and Adrian's *Four Cities*, suggests that city governments might be classified under four heads according to their political preoccupations or styles.[16] These are city governments chiefly devoted to promoting economic development; to providing and securing life's amenities for the citizens; merely to maintaining traditional services; and to arbitrating among conflicting interests. While these particular categories reflect the range of choices of stance open to American cities and cannot be said to apply more than very crudely in England, it is possible to discern the outlines of different stances among the four county boroughs of Merseyside. Birkenhead's low rate and underdeveloped service position has already been noted, as has Bootle's preoccupation with its economic future. Wallasey has been, generally, a good provider of services and amenities, but the scale of its needs in relation to its resources has been comparatively less burdensome. Liverpool, the giant of the four, but with giant problems, could be expected to show a more varied and complex political pattern, as befits a big city. Variations in the nature and focus of party conflict from town to town could also be expected. Some might show a higher element of class conflict than others. Party conflict might be acerbic in some but not in others.

In the next two chapters we shall examine how the different political styles of the four boroughs were reflected in the newspapers, and what contribution they themselves made to them.

# 5
## Press content analysed

The agenda of local government and politics at any point in time is largely a product of the past history, geographical location, social and economic composition of the community. These produce a particular pattern of needs which local government has to try to meet. Much of the resultant activity is of a routine, uncontroversial nature. From time to time, however, there will be matters of controversy, involving newly perceived needs, questions of priority, or conflicts between different values. In an advanced form, these become 'issues'. What becomes an 'issue' and how it is treated is largely determined by the interplay in any one place of parties, pressures and personalities. The process of perceiving needs and fitting responses to them is one which goes on all the time; it has been routinised over many years, and built upon by layers of incremental decision-making. What creates a stir takes place against this background.

Newspaper coverage reflects all of these elements of the local scene. But it does so in ways which are peculiar to the newspaper itself. The newspaper has its own needs. It makes its own interpretation of the political world it is covering. Thus the image of the local political scene which the reader gets will be a product both of what has actually been going on and of what the newspaper, for its part, has made of it. In this chapter we attempt to convey, largely in statistical terms, what exact amount, type and proportion of news of local government and politics the six papers conveyed in the 1960s. In the subsequent chapter we shall attempt to put flesh on this by some accounts of actual treatment.

In the light of what is emphasised above of the on-going nature of local government's work, to concentrate on 'issues' to the exclusion of the more routine coverage of local government would be false both to the nature of the system and to the nature of press coverage. What is needed is, therefore, to evolve a method of content analysis which is adapted to the idea of politics and government as a system, and which enables us also to carry out a comparative examination of papers' coverage of it over a fairly lengthy period of time.

### PRESS COVERAGE OF POLITICS: A SYSTEMS MODEL

Political scientists have found it convenient to view political life as a system, whereby a range of 'inputs' such as demands, resources, and supports are addressed to a decision-taking 'core' and are ultimately processed into 'outputs' such as legislation, budgetary allocations and other decisions. What we have attempted to do here is to create and operationalise a simple model along these lines for the purpose of analysing newspaper content. Different types of coverage are seen as representing these inputs and outputs as the newspaper reflects them and contributes to them. Let us be clear that the items of information carried in the newspaper about inputs and outputs are not those actions themselves, for these take place in the whole sphere of political life and not just in newsprint. But neither are they mere mirrors of these actions. The newspaper's work is part of the action, in some cases manifestly so.

We may, then, divide news coverage into two broad categories, inputs and outputs, distinguished by the meaning of their message vis-à-vis the decision-making and administrative core of the system, sometimes popularly referred to as 'the authorities'. Inputs consist of messages which contain, in essence, interest articulation – in other words demands upon the system core for action of some kind; and also supportive statements proffered to it. These may be various in type, ranging from the general 'they're doing a poor/grand job', to specific demands and supports relating to a policy or action of current concern. Outputs consist of messages containing news of action taking place which emanates from the system core, i.e. the making, applying or adjudication of rules, together with information which helps to give the background to those actions or helps citizens to adjust their lives to changes resulting from them. But, to repeat, the newspaper does not merely *reflect* political messages generated in its fields of surveillance. It may itself, through its comment (not to mention its news selection), be an active participant at any point in the process, offering its own support or expressing and stimulating demands.

We may, therefore, further sub-divide these input and output categories into respectively, four and two further divisions. Inputs are of four types – demands and supports which the paper reports; and those which it presents itself. Outputs are of two types, which we might term news of events, and background information.

It should be noted that not only do demands and supports range over a wide spectrum from the most general to the most specific, but also that at any one time the system core, the 'authorities', may be assailed by a range of contradictory demands. On a particular issue one group may demand an action, while another demands a different action or none at all. The purpose of singling out such categories as 'demand' from the corpus of news coverage is not to demonstrate the rightness or wrongness of a particular policy, but its controversiality. Demand is taken as an indication that public opinion, at any rate as reflected in press coverage, is engaged on a particular issue, and that the authority's action, or lack of it, is a matter of concern.

We would naturally expect a relatively much smaller proportion of coverage to fall into the 'support' categories. Expressions of bland, uncritical support are not common and usually not newsworthy. If a speech is made or a letter written it is naturally the critical or suggestive parts which are likely to prove of interest to readers, and to be given the papers' attention. In practice if there is going to be unreserved praise for any local government action it is likely in most cases to be the paper itself which gives it. Hence, while we must leave open the theoretical possibility of 'supports reported', in practice this category covers such a small number of cases that it will be convenient to omit it.

There are, thus, six potential, five actual, divisions into which an item of coverage may fall (Table 4). The largest category, naturally, consists of the basic, bread and butter 'news', or 'events' taking

Table 4. *Categories of news coverage*

| A. Inputs | | | |
|---|---|---|---|
| I. Demands reported | II. Demands expressed by paper | IIIa. Supports reported | IIIb. Supports expressed by paper |

| B. Outputs | |
|---|---|
| I. 'News', i.e. events reported | II. Information |

48

place involving the political system and its ramifications (B.I). Some of these may be further differentiated, however, as the main significance is a demand for an action, or stance to be adopted (A.I). Then there are demands expressed by the paper itself (A.II), and supports offered by it (A.III), usually in editorials. There is also the virtually nil category of supports reported by the paper (A.IIIa). Lastly, there is an important service of information and background, largely, though not invariably, given in feature articles (B.II).

Such a division must be somewhat arbitrary, and this indeed is a primary reason for not adopting a more complicated one. But the vast bulk of coverage does fit unambiguously into one or other of these six divisions. The items in which the main thrust of the 'message' conveyed is *not* a straightforward one – e.g. an editorial in which praise and criticism is of *equal* weight, are comparatively few. In an earlier chapter it was noted that the local newspaper, in contrast with the national newspaper, is generally unable to use the specialist reporter whose reportage of 'what happened' or 'what was said', becomes a set piece in which his own evaluative, and perhaps frankly partisan, gloss is imposed on the material. The local reader is more likely to read 'what was said' in its raw, verbatim state. The relative simplicity of the world of the local paper enables the researcher to engage in a comprehensive study of coverage while keeping within the bounds of manageability.

We may best illustrate our schema by reference to a typical, hypothetical case. In recent years many councils have embarked upon central redevelopment schemes. In the output category, therefore, we should place any 'news' concerning intention to start such a scheme, or news of the progress of the construction and opening of the development. Such news would consist of items like speeches and statements announcing the proposed scheme, more as it gradually approached the stage of commencement of building, a periodic photographic glimpse of the work in progress, and a 'splash' story at the time of opening. All this, being news of an event in train, would be classified under B.I. There are likely to be occasions when the paper prints information which relates to the scheme independently of any specific event. It may print a layout plan, a timetable of the stages by which the work is expected to be completed, or a feature article on some aspect of the background of the scheme. Few large schemes are opened without being marked by a general special supplement in addition to straight news reportage.

This is not 'news' as such but is an aid to the understanding of news, or essential information citizens may appreciate as an aid in their daily affairs. All this may be categorised under B.II. Inputs relating to the scheme would include demands that it be undertaken in the first place, as well as demands that it be *not* undertaken. Some at least of the potential gainers and losers would have had their views reported in the paper, or would have used the paper directly as a means of expressing their hopes or fears through giving interviews or writing letters to the editor. Then, during the actual progress of building and opening, there may be 'demands' arising from the harmful or potentially beneficial effect of the scheme on particular groups. These might include the grievances of traders unable to pay new rents or compete with multiple stores enjoying the benefit of new premises. In many cases the political parties themselves may be expected to act as articulators of demand. There is enormous scope for condemnation of redevelopment schemes as spendthrift, foolhardy, grandiose, betraying a wrong sense of priorities, etc., etc. It is hardly to be wondered at that few schemes have not had this kind of attendant publicity from some at least of the local politicians. Demands, then, of various types, may be reported by the paper (A.I). Finally, we must note that the paper will have its own view to put forward, and usually, though not exclusively, the editorial column is the vehicle for this type of coverage. Occasionally this is used as a further means of giving information purely and simply (B.II). But it is more usual for the paper to support the 'authorities' (A.IIIb) or to voice criticism, i.e. demand (A.II).

## PROBLEMS OF APPLICATION

In the survey of newspaper content which is reported on subsequent pages this analytic scheme was applied to the six Merseyside papers in respect of their coverage of local government and politics during the 1960s. The analysis is based upon a reading of the papers for the years 1962–9 inclusively. The four weekly papers were read in their entirety, while a 5 per cent sample of the dailies, adjusted slightly to take account of the seasons of the political year (August being a very slack month for political news) was read. For the purposes of the detailed content analysis of local political coverage, it was convenient to take the two dailies together, as if they were morning and evening editions of the one paper. They were products of the one house, the work of the one organisation; and they appeared to overlap quite often in the news items printed. The basis of the survey was the simple presence of a news item or mention. This is not significantly less reliable, for most purposes, than the infinitely more troublesome method of counting column-inches. The proportion of mentions which are small snippets of, say, less than 5 column-inches, to those which are more substantial or have eye-catching headlines, has a bearing on the nature of coverage and is also dealt with in the discussion. Any single entry in the paper which dealt with any aspect of local government and politics was counted as a mention. This included photographs, editorials and letters to the editor. Each separate 'piece' was counted, even if it dealt with a topic already mentioned elsewhere in the paper. Where a lengthier item mentioned more than one service, or more than one functional category of coverage type was involved (neither of these occurred very frequently) separate 'mentions' were recorded. Reference is made subsequently to the coverage given in the daily papers to the affairs of the three smaller boroughs. In the case of the latter, reference to matters beyond the borough boundary was not frequent and was ignored. As we have said, classification presented fewer difficult decisions than might have been expected, owing to the nature of most coverage. Readers' letters were perhaps the most ambiguous type of coverage, since they were neither the voice of the paper nor the result of reportage. However, a demand expressed in a letter has the same effect as one in a reported speech; and the same applies to news and information contained in them. Any distortions caused by the nature of the schema and the occasional decisions it imposed were no greater, and in most cases were less, than those which are accepted as reasonable hazards of the enterprise in questionnaire-based surveys or studies based on the manipulation of statistics.

## POLITICS AND THE WHOLE NEWSPAPER

Before we look at the coverage of local politics by local newspapers, attention must be given to the interrelated problems of the availability of news and the frequency of appearance of the newspaper.

The activities of the political parties, voluntary associations, the council and local administration provides a basic flow of information which varies over periods of time and from one town to another. Some of this information journalists treat as 'news' and publish; much of it never sees the light of day. What becomes 'news' is partly a product of senior journalists' definition of 'news', a problem discussed earlier and further examined in chapter 7. A very important element in the journalist's attitude to news finding and publicising, is the number of opportunities he has to go to press, i.e. whether he is on a weekly, bi-weekly or a daily. Urgency to meet deadlines on a daily is normal, whereas on a weekly it becomes a problem only when a 'story' threatens to 'break' just as the paper goes to press. The weekly journalist has to accept such things and see his normal function as nearer that of the weekly magazine which provides a survey of the news of the past week, some of which may have been publicised elsewhere, and some of which, by the standards of a daily, is stale by the time it gets printed.

The weekly journalist operates under the umbrella of daily press, T.V. and radio coverage, part of which will cover his particular local 'beat'. Frequency of appearance, and the umbrella role of other media, help frame his awareness of his job.

Comparisons, then, between the content of weeklies within a conurbation and the daily papers of the whole conurbation should be seen in this light. The four Merseyside county boroughs are served by three weeklies, one bi-weekly (the *Birkenhead News*) and the two dailies. Each daily paper has six times the opportunity for printing news that a weekly has, and three times that of a bi-weekly. In Liverpool, for example, the two dailies, in their Liverpool editions have, together, twelve times more opportunity of coverage than has the *Liverpool Weekly News*. Even if the daily coverage of local politics in the *Liverpool Echo* were small it would be likely, cumulatively over one week, to exceed in volume that provided by the *Liverpool Weekly News*.

The differential opportunity to publish, however, is only one factor among several. At least two other factors reduce the difference between the total coverage of local politics given by daily and by weekly papers. Firstly there is the supply of news. Journalists appear to act as if high news value material is scarce. Even the weeklies run short of it at times. Hence the urge on the part of the dailies to spread it around more thinly, over a fairly wide range of topics and districts, trying to avoid too much repetition between morning and evening paper.

Secondly, there is the focus of the daily papers. Even in their local editions the papers are not just Liverpool papers. The degree to which the Northwest in general and certainly the whole conurbation is their beat is easily demonstrated. A sample of their coverage reveals that 18·7 per cent – nearly one fifth – of their total coverage of local – as opposed to national – government and politics is specifically devoted to the affairs of one or other of the three other county boroughs (see Table 6). In addition to this, a further 10 per cent is devoted to problems of conurbation-wide interest, e.g. the various motorway schemes, the new Mersey tunnel, etc. Let us illustrate this by a slight digression to examine the dailies' editorial areas of concern. The sample revealed that of those editorials devoted to local or 'Merseyside' matters 57 per cent were devoted to Liverpool, 23 per cent dealt specifically with one or other of the three boroughs and 20 per cent with 'Merseyside' matters. Nearly a third, then, of total coverage of local politics and nearly half of editorials was given by the dailies to matters beyond the city of Liverpool. The morning *Post*, particularly, maintained a regional outlook. The editorial column often did not refer to local affairs for several weeks, and any comments were usually on the 'big' issues of conurbation-wide concern. A fairly normal seven days was that beginning Saturday 1 February 1964. The *Post*'s editorials that week were as follows:

1 February: Missiles; holiday facilities.
3 February: The proposed second Mersey tunnel; temperance; national politics.
4 February: The proposed second Mersey tunnel; the law.
5 February: The Liberal party and Wales.
6 February: Cyprus; good behaviour.
7 February: A Channel tunnel? the privilege of M.P.s

Local affairs were thus dealt with on two days. The negotiations on a proposed new tunnel were at an important stage, and the *Post*'s message, in essence, was, 'Birkenhead, stop holding us all up'. In the first week of August of 1964 there was a similar spread of topics – Russia and the United Nations; going to the moon; bank holiday traffic; law and order. Only one editorial dealt with a local issue; on the Thursday the second leader dealt briefly with traffic conditions in Birkenhead.

The *Liverpool Echo* did not in this period carry what would be recognised immediately as an editorial column. But in its feature page it contained a column 'Echoes and Gossip of the Day', performing the same function. Here its surveillance was much more intensively local. A majority of issues carried an item in this column concerning some facets of Merseyside local government responsibility. In the first week of August 1966, the *Echo* editorialised on the following issues:

1 August: Willaston (a green belt village); Burma.
2 August: The Gateacre line (a suburban line in Liverpool threatened with closure); the Bootle Police (to be merged with Liverpool's).
3 August: Redeveloment in Liverpool; car stealing.
4 August: The Territorial Army; the police (a general paragraph in support of).
5 August: Transport (rising fares); the B.B.C.; the National Debt.
6 August: The Inland Revenue; traffic in Bootle.

This was a fairly typical week's spread. In the equivalent week two years earlier the topics covered had included road deaths; the dangerous state of the canal in Bootle; buses; and a small item on Liverpool's Georgian town hall.

'Liverpool only' coverage, then, while it has, potentially, more room to compete *for* in the dailies, has also much more news to compete *with*. Conversely, of course, these figures illustrate the extent of the daily 'umbrella' under which the weeklies operate. For their part they devote little or no space to affairs beyond their town boundaries.

The results from a 5 per cent sample of total contents during the 1960s are shown in Table 5. Advertisements – without which papers simply could not appear – take up between a quarter and over half, on average 40 per cent, of the total space. All other news and information competes for entry into just over half the paper.

Of what is left, most is not 'news' either. There is the routine, but valued, publicity of births, marriages and deaths. Marriages, particularly, provide very useful, easily obtainable, copy of direct local interest. Sport provides regular copy, both popular and accessible. So, too, do regular features such as the women's and children's pages, occasional articles on local places and worthies, and material in the general area of 'human interest'. The proportion of space given to these sections remains fairly constant; they have reader appeal though they rarely make the front page. What does do so and provides the headlines, the big pictures – the initial impact of a paper – is news. Whatever else this might consist of, it certainly contains some news of local politicians and Town Hall.

Table 5. *Total content by type (column-inches)*
(*5 per cent sample; 1962–69 inclusive*)

| | Total news % | News % | | Sport % | Ads % | Features % | Births, marriages, deaths % | Column-inches per paper |
| | | a (news other than polit-ical) | b (polit-ical news) | | | | | |
|---|---|---|---|---|---|---|---|---|
| *Wallasey N.* | 16·7 | 9·3 | 7·4 | 9·2 | 60·8 | 9·7 | 2·8 | 2,570 |
| *Birkenhead N.* | 23·1 | 17·5 | 5·6 | 13·8 | 47·4 | 11·6 | 3·9 | 3,136 |
| *Bootle T.H.* | 30·0 | 23·3 | 6·7 | 11·6 | 37·1 | 16·6 | 4·3 | 2,036 |
| *Liverpool W.N.* | 24·2 | 18·4 | 5·8 | 18·8 | 42·8 | 14·1 | 2·1 | 2,381 |
| *Liverpool D.P.* | 34·6 | 32·8 | 1·8 | 15·2 | 26·2 | 20·9 | 0·6 | 2,549 |
| *Liverpool E.* | 26·5 | 24·7 | 1·8 | 6·8 | 44·6 | 12·7 | 3·6 | 2,910 |

A glance at Table 5 reveals that when compared with their counterparts in other newspapers, the degree of variation between the sizes of these sections is considerable among the weeklies, and increases greatly when the dailies are included. The news area is no exception, some papers having twice as much news as others. The coverage of local politics should be seen against this background. In percentage terms local politics averages only 6 per cent of total column-inches in the weeklies and just over 4 per cent overall, if the dailies are included. To look at it this way is, of course, misleading. When compared with the total volume of news, the 'newshole', what happens in local politics does seem to have news appeal. In the Birkenhead, Bootle and Liverpool weeklies politics seems to provide about a quarter of total news coverage, while in Wallasey the proportion is almost a half. In the case of the latter, it is also noteworthy that advertisements in Wallasey take up 60·8 per cent of column inches – well over the average, in fact, for this group of newspapers. Increased advertisement in Wallasey appears to accompany a smaller proportion of features and general news rather than political news, compared with the other weeklies.

Advertisements leave half the paper's coverage to be apportioned, and routine cover of sports, features and births, marriages and deaths consumes over half this space, leaving all news, including the political, to fill the remaining 20–25 per cent. The immediate competitor with political news, then is other 'current news' – crime, human interest stories and so on. Any expansion of the size of the paper, for whatever reason, would mean, *prima facie*, more space available not simply for news but for *all* sections of the paper. In other words, the competition between news areas would not simply be abated with bigger newspapers.

News concerning local government and politics is, then, a small part of the total space in the local newspaper, even after the advertisements have been excluded. It is, however, a not inconsiderable quarter to a half of the news coverage in the weeklies. In the dailies – even allowing for their much wider field of coverage – the proportion is less than a quarter. What exactly does this political news consist of? We may analyse it according to a number of criteria. How much of the attention is devoted to local authority services and how much to party politics? What *kind* of coverage is given to local politics – that is to say, how much is given to demands, supports, straight news, information, and so on? How is coverage distributed between the several fields of local authority responsibility?

## PRESS COVERAGE OF LOCAL GOVERNMENT

While all of the four county boroughs provide the basic local authority services, some provide unique services, such as Liverpool with its airport, Wallasey with the New Brighton seaside resort, and some cooperate in joint ventures such as the running of the Mersey Tunnel. Thus a distinction has to be drawn between newspaper coverage of services common to all, and their coverage of the rest. There is thus the tripartite division of coverage shown in Table 6 – coverage of services common to all four boroughs, coverage of unique services and coverage of general local political life such as party politics, civic dignitaries and so on.

Most items of local politics in the local newspaper concern the administration of the various services. The figure for the dailies is that for Liverpool services and is lowered by their wider focus, some one-fifth of their local political coverage being of politics in the other three boroughs. The *Liverpool Weekly News* is exceptionally concerned with covering services (87 per cent) but less concerned with party politics or with Liverpool's special services. The three other weeklies give 70 per cent of their coverage to local services. Birkenhead, Liverpool and Wallasey were, in the 1960s, much concerned with the problems of easy travel into and within the conurbation. Thus, much newspaper attention was focused on the projected new Mersey tunnel, the creation of new approaches

Table 6. *Total coverage of local government and politics, 1962–69*

| Type of political coverage | L.D.P. & L.E. $n=477$ (sample) | L.W.N. $n=2111$ | B.T.H. $n=2022$ | W.N. $n=2932$ | B.N. $n=3086$ |
|---|---|---|---|---|---|
| | % | % | % | % | % |
| Services common to all | 60·4 | 87·0 | 75·0 | 71·3 | 68·5 |
| Unique services | 8·8 | 1·5 | 0·2 | 10·1 | 8·4 |
| General politics, etc. | 12·1 | 11·5 | 24·8 | 18·6 | 23·1 |
| Non-Liverpool | 18·7 | 0 | N.A. | N.A. | N.A. |

L.D.P. & L.E. = *Liverpool Daily Post*, and *Liverpool Echo*
L.W.N.        = *Liverpool Weekly News*
B.T.H.        = *Bootle Times Herald*
W.N.          = *Wallasey News*
B.N.          = *Birkenhead News*

to both it and the existing one, the proposed Wirral motorway, proposals for, and the ultimate creation of, a Passenger Transport Authority, and so on. In the case of Wallasey the problem arising from the decline of New Brighton as a holiday resort was another important source of news. By separating out these services which are not comparable we see the peculiar concerns of individual parts of Merseyside, as well as their participation in common problems. In particular the barrier of the Mersey estuary made the hazards of transport and the hope of improvement a constant source of news for all.

The remainder of the coverage is mostly given over to party political news. This is a substantial category in its own right, being nearly a quarter of all political news in the *Birkenhead News* and *Bootle Times Herald*, averaging some 18 per cent over all the weeklies and exceeding 10 per cent in the dailies. Quite apart from the coverage gained by local politicians in relation to public services it is clear that their doings and utterances formed valuable news for journalists.

On the one hand there was civic news – the coverage of the civic round of mayoral visits and receptions for important guests. And there was party news – adoptions of candidates, meetings for social as well as political purposes, and so on. From February onwards there was election campaign news, which usually was worth quite considerable, if largely factual and photographic, coverage.

There were other chances of publicity too. Politicians are apt to complain that journalists too often prefer to cover the gossipy showman politician than the less publicity conscious, but worthy, loyal party man who is doing a good job. Certainly in each town one or two councillors seemed to corner a great deal of the publicity.

During the period Bootle and Liverpool, in particular, sought to refurbish their national images. In Liverpool a new Public Relations Department worked with the *Liverpool Daily Post* and the *Liverpool Echo* to publicise the 'new' Liverpool. In Bootle, it is clear that the newspaper actively promoted publicity campaigns – the Borough was twinned with Mons in Belgium and this event, and the town's centenary celebrations were boosted by vigorous publicity. Judged by press publicity Birkenhead was more quietly twinned. Bootle also loudly and colourfully 'Backed Britain' when opportunity offered. Thus the newspapers obtained easy copy from the various civic doings, featuring mayors and other leading politicians, and some politicians secured very easy publicity. Local party politics and politicians may not rate so much news in total, but it is they who frequently provide the front page lead story and much of the 'gossip'.

In the rest of this chapter we concentrate on the coverage of services common to all four boroughs; and in analysing it, Table 7 makes use of the method outlined earlier, namely the input–output

Table 7. *Newspaper coverage of services common to all, by functional category*

| | A.I % | A.II % | A.IIIb % | B.I % | B.II % | No. of mentions |
|---|---|---|---|---|---|---|
| *Liverpool W.N.* | 46·1 | 3·2 | 1·8 | 43.0 | 8·9 | 1,861 |
| *Wallasey N.* | 25·8 | 2·6 | 5·5 | 60·2 | 5·8 | 2,091 |
| *Bootle T.H.* | 18·6 | 3·1 | 5·8 | 66·3 | 6·2 | 1,517 |
| *Birkenhead N.* | 25·9 | 3·2 | 6·9 | 58·0 | 5·9 | 2,115 |
| *Liverpool D.P.* ⎫ *Liverpool E.* ⎭ | 19·4 | 5·5 | 5·2 | 55·2 | 14·6 | 288 (5% sample) |

model. To recapitulate, demands reported by the papers go into the A.I category, while reports and editorials clearly aimed at stimulating public response go in A.II. Reports and features of a clearly supportive character go in A.IIIb. News and information, B.I and B.II, are distinguished by immediacy, B.II being essentially background information.

The obvious preponderance of straightforward 'news' items about people and events in politics – our category B.I – is only to be expected. This is the base from which all else deviates. The exception is the *Liverpool Weekly News*. In the publicising of specific demands on the political system – Category A.I – the *Liverpool Weekly News* quite clearly marks itself off from the other papers. Since such publicity is a special type of news – categories A.I and B.I jointly constitute news – it can be said that over a half of *Liverpool Weekly News* news items appear in the form of demands for action of one sort or another. By contrast in the other papers this category is much more like a quarter or a third of their news.

The other types of coverage are also illuminating. It seems clear that the papers see themselves as stimulating opinion, if at all, largely indirectly via front-paging and layout. They confine themselves to one, or at most two, editorials per week on local political topics in the dailies, or per month in the weeklies, and this obviously keeps down the total *numbers* of demands stimulated. In this area the otherwise strident *Liverpool Weekly News* is no different and the non-crusading *Liverpool Daily Post* and the *Echo* are somewhat exceptional. The newspapers in general carry comparatively little that is supportive (A.III) or educational and informative (B.II) regarding local politics and administration. The Liverpool papers' performance in these categories is revealing. The *Liverpool Weekly News* is a vehicle for strident demands, offers little 'support' yet chooses to keep its *own* voice sotto voce. The *Liverpool Daily Post* and the *Liverpool Echo* by contrast are more the 'insiders' papers taking 'responsible' positions, encouraging their readers to do the same and supplying them with soberly presented information. They are not vehicles for minority demands or for sensation seekers. Put briefly, one might say, the *Liverpool Weekly News* shouts 'needs' and the *Liverpool Daily Post* and the *Liverpool Echo* speak soberly of 'resources', necessities', 'principles'.

## SOME SELECTED SERVICES

The different emphases of the newspapers in covering local politics may be termed their political styles. While a paper's political style may be detected in outline in the overall figures, it is even more clearly seen in the treatment of different local authority services. At the same time, as was noted in chapter 4, the different sizes, class and population structures and economic characteristics of the four boroughs lead to somewhat different preoccupations and approaches to problems. This, as well as the papers' political styles, must be related to coverage.

An exhaustive analysis of newspaper coverage, service by service, is not necessary to bring out the different towns' problems and the different newspaper styles. In Table 8 we have selected some of those services which, being big consumers of revenue and of wide-ranging impact, habitually receive a greater degree of attention, and some that are 'smaller' and more unobtrusive, such as the personal services. Before the revised committee structures were introduced in the late 1960s following the Maud report and Liverpool's own McKinsey report, we could broadly say that there was one committee per service area, though there were minor

Table 8. *Coverage of selected services, by functional category, (%) 1962–69*

|  | A.I | A.II | A.IIIb | B.I | B.II | % of common service total | Mentions N |
|---|---|---|---|---|---|---|---|
| **Education** | | | | | | | |
| L.W.N. | 17·6 | 2·9 | 0·4 | 76·1 | 2·9 | 18·3 | 342 |
| W.N. | 20·9 | 2·8 | 3·7 | 60·2 | 12·5 | 16·8 | 352 |
| B.T.H. | 11·8 | 2·7 | 5·0 | 73·3 | 6·1 | 24·6 | 374 |
| B.N. | 20·8 | 1·6 | 5·5 | 63·0 | 9·1 | 18·1 | 384 |
| L.D.P. ⎫ *&* L.E. ⎭ | 22·7 | 0 | 0 | 77·3 | 0 | 7·6 | 22 (sample) |
| **Housing** | | | | | | | |
| L.W.N. | 61·4 | 5·3 | 0·5 | 25·8 | 7·0 | 30·6 | 571 |
| W.N. | 27·7 | 3·4 | 4·5 | 61·6 | 2·8 | 8·5 | 177 |
| B.T.H. | 34·3 | 6·1 | 4·3 | 53·5 | 1·7 | 15·2 | 230 |
| B.N. | 39·1 | 1·4 | 5·3 | 51·2 | 2·9 | 7·8 | 207 |
| L.D.P. ⎫ *&* L.E. ⎭ | 28·9 | 6·7 | 4·4 | 42·2 | 17·8 | 15·6 | 45 (sample) |

| | A.I | A.II | A.IIIb | B.I | B.II | % of common service total | Mentions N |
|---|---|---|---|---|---|---|---|
| **Planning** | | | | | | | |
| L.W.N. | 57·9 | 5·3 | 0·3 | 31·3 | 5·3 | 10·2 | 190 |
| W.N. | 23·1 | 2·9 | 4·1 | 65·7 | 4·1 | 11·6 | 242 |
| B.T.H. | 13·3 | 1·5 | 8·2 | 62·6 | 14·3 | 12·8 | 195 |
| B.N. | 37·8 | 2·9 | 7·3 | 48·6 | 6·4 | 16·3 | 344 |
| L.D.P. & L.E. | 21·3 | 6·4 | 0 | 46·8 | 25·5 | 16·3 | 47 (sample) |
| **Highways** | | | | | | | |
| L.W.N. | 77·8 | 0 | 0·7 | 21·5 | 0 | 9·7 | 182 |
| W.N. | 27·0 | 3·4 | 5·0 | 61·2 | 3·4 | 8·5 | 178 |
| B.T.H. | 37·9 | 2·6 | 0·9 | 56·9 | 1·7 | 7·6 | 116 |
| B.N. | 34·4 | 5·7 | 6·1 | 50·3 | 3·4 | 14·0 | 296 |
| L.D.P. & L.E. | 11·9 | 7·1 | 7·1 | 59·5 | 14·3 | 14·6 | 42 (sample) |
| **Public transport** | | | | | | | |
| L.W.N. | 20·0 | 0 | 0·7 | 59·3 | 20·0 | 2·7 | 51 |
| W.N. | 41·6 | 3·4 | 2·6 | 48·7 | 3·7 | 18·2 | 380 |
| B.T.H. | 48·6 | 5·7 | 2·8 | 42·8 | 0 | 2·3 | 35 |
| B.N. | 27·0 | 4·7 | 5·9 | 58·8 | 3·5 | 12·0 | 255 |
| L.D.P. & L.E. | 25·8 | 9·7 | 3·2 | 58·1 | 3·2 | 10·8 | 31 (sample) |
| **Police** | | | | | | | |
| L.W.N. | 37·5 | 12·5 | 0·4 | 37·1 | 12·5 | 4·3 | 80 |
| W.N. | 12·7 | 1·1 | 11·8 | 66·8 | 7·7 | 8·6 | 181 |
| B.T.H. | 13·6 | 3·1 | 12·3 | 64·8 | 6·2 | 10·7 | 162 |
| B.N. | 9·1 | 1·2 | 11·6 | 72·6 | 5·4 | 11·4 | 241 |
| L.D.P. & L.E. | 3·1 | 3·1 | 18·7 | 68·7 | 6·2 | 11·1 | 32 (sample) |
| **Children and welfare** | | | | | | | |
| L.W.N. | 43·7 | 6·3 | 0·1 | 33·4 | 16·2 | 9·8 | 182 |
| W.N. | 20·1 | 0·9 | 7·4 | 70·6 | 0·9 | 3·1 | 65 |
| B.T.H. | 7·9 | 0 | 2·5 | 85·3 | 4·2 | 3·7 | 57 |
| B.N. | 15·0 | 8·3 | 6·6 | 60·9 | 10·0 | 2·8 | 60 |
| L.D.P. & L.E. | 0 | 0 | 0 | 12·5 | 87·5 | 1·7 | 5 (sample) |

differences from borough to borough. In order to obtain uniformity of analysis we have concentrated on the services themselves regardless of the committee structures governing them.

Education as a service provided much copy and was clearly seen as highly newsworthy in the decade of the comprehensive schools issue. The basic news, the routine coverage of education, took the form of school news – examination results, prize day speeches, new buildings etc. The three weeklies in the smaller boroughs, in particular, covered exhaustively all the major prize days, and usually printed the entire G.C.E. results for the town. Bootle, in particular, a town with a birth rate well above average, appeared to be very primary school conscious. Feature pages were devoted to different schools in the town, including a page of photographs from each school. The absence of this type of coverage from the dailies accounts in large measure for their seemingly lesser attention to education. There was also periodic coverage of council and committee consideration of the education budget. When the comprehensive school question became contentious, this routine coverage was supplemented by council and committee debates and reports, the claims and counter-claims of spokesmen for parents and teacher's associations, letters, background articles on past and likely future government policy and so on. In a subsequent chapter the contrasting styles of approach to this controversy are described.

Such was the substance of education news. The impact of controversy on coverage is clearly seen in the figures. The weeklies devoted in the 1960s nearly a sixth of their total service coverage to education. They and the dailies provided more news and much more information on this than on any other topic, and they recorded a considerable volume of demands on the local authorities. The comprehensive question was clearly seen by journalists as requiring delicate handling. The *Liverpool Weekly News*, compared to its style on other services, published a smaller proportion of demands for action and, judged by its background information effort, seemed uncharacteristically detached from the whole affair. The *Wallasey News* stood in some contrast to the *Liverpool Weekly News* in being notably more informative, and all three borough weeklies were more continually supportive of the policy makers.

Housing, likewise, provided much controversy in the 1960s. The normal run of items usually consisted of announcements of planned new council estates, items on their building and opening and criticisms of deficiencies. In addition there was coverage of housing policy, budgetary arguments, one or two pieces on poverty and bad housing, accompanied by appropriate illustrations. Clearly, after 1967, a 'news area' for journalists was the question of sale of council houses to tenants, government attitudes to this and local reactions to changes of policy.

The differences in the *ways* in which housing news was presented by the papers is striking as are the differences in amounts of coverage. The range of total coverage between the papers was greater than in the case of education, the *Liverpool Weekly News* devoting nearly a third of its total coverage of all services to housing. The *Weekly News* had probably the worst housed readership of the six papers; in addition, it made it its business to give voice occasionally to the bitter cry of outcast Liverpool. The level of demands of one kind or another reported by the papers was high – averaging nearly a third of their housing coverage and, for the *Liverpool Weekly News*, nearly two-thirds. Housing, like education, was a large subject, but it was in some respects a safer subject for a reader-conscious paper to take a stand on. Bad housing could be treated as a communal Merseyside problem, a 'legacy' from the past, no one's 'fault'. Only the *Liverpool Weekly News* occasionally dissented from this view. The *Wallasey News*, in the best housed borough, was relatively less concerned with housing, and, for example, gave it less than half the attention it gave to public transport. The Liverpool papers were more active in stimulating their readers on housing than they were on education. Not only was this so in front-paging and editorialising, but also in the amount of background information which was supplied – a very considerable amount in the case of the dailies.

There was considerable overlap between the coverage given to the related services of planning and 'highways', i.e. traffic engineering, road building etc. in the 1960s. Such coverage dealt in the main with the gradual implementation of plans for urban redevelopment, encompassing new shopping centres and amenities as well as industrial sites and the improving or provision of new road networks. News of the outcomes of applications for planning permission by individuals and small firms provided an ample source of small snippets for use as 'fillers'. The strains inherent in the displacing of people and business of all kinds and the disruption of communities, all formed news areas for journalists. The coverage in the *Liverpool Weekly News* distinctly exhibited a very clear pattern – a high level of reported demands and no support given to the policy makers. The dailies provided the most background information and were the most active in stimulating their readers by editorialising and front paging. Both Wallasey and Birkenhead papers carried a fairly high level of demands though, judged by coverage, the strains were greater in the latter town. The major redevelopment schemes of Bootle, on the other hand, were carried out in a general atmosphere of approval, and gave rise to less continuing controversy than did highway development. The *Bootle Times Herald* normally gave at least average support to policy makers compared with the rest – the area of highways being a noticeable exception.

Public transport services everywhere were news and sometimes very big news. In this area especially, the impact of particular, non-routine, one-off events on the life of a town was most reflected in the local press (the figures for the dailies being based on a sample, fail to show this). Strikes, transport economies and their consequences formed the bulk of public transport news in the 1960s. The interaction of falling revenues, rising fares, service cuts, labour disputes, along with moves towards the creation of a Passenger Transport Authority, ensured transport services steady and sometimes considerable coverage. Liverpool and Birkenhead both had bus strikes, that in Liverpool lasting for eight weeks. In Wallasey the Conservative-controlled council's effort to rationalise and economise on the bus services led to widespread and often acrimonious debate, which the *Wallasey News* covered thoroughly. The *Wallasey News* devoted more space to public transport than to education or to any other service and, within that coverage, vented a higher level of public demands than on any other subject. Its letters column was extensively used for this purpose. The paper was clearly read by a large number of highly articulate, and irritated, commuters. Significantly its miscellany column was called 'Talk on the Boats' – a reference to the ferry services to and from Liverpool.

The *Birkenhead News* gave more room to public transport than to housing and recorded more public demands on the subject than, for example, on education. Clearly, public transport service costs, cuts and strikes evoked an immediate public response in a way that change in other services, causing less *immediate* effect, could not. Bootle did not have a separate transport service and the paper gave transport little attention, except when a strike or rationalisation in Liverpool led to increased coverage and the expression of anti-Liverpool sentiments. The Liverpool papers may again be contrasted. The *Liverpool Weekly News* gave small coverage to this topic and, given its norm, vented surprisingly low levels of public demand. The Liverpool dailies devoted a great deal of attention to the strike, recorded a higher level of demands than on education and were noticeably active in stimulating demands by front-paging and editorialising.

In contrast, the police service was much more routinely covered. The courts, of course, provided plenty of easily available copy, but this was not counted as coverage of the police as such. Typically, such coverage consisted of organisational changes such as the Bootle – Liverpool police merger, of promotions and of background information on police activity in the 'war on crime'. The overall volume of coverage was substantial, save in the *Liverpool Weekly News*. There, what coverage there was followed the paper's habitual stance and implied a much higher level of public demand, e.g. on the failure to stop vandalism and theft, than did the other papers, and, equally, it was more active in stimulating such demands. The police were clearly seen by the other papers as worthy of fairly continuous support, the dailies giving nearly a fifth of their police coverage to items praising police efforts. The *Liverpool Weekly News* was neither so generous nor so interested.

The children's and welfare services are included as an example of services receiving very small coverage. Normally this consisted of a few minor items mainly about the costs of the services and occasional new developments such as the opening of centres. When combined – the *Liverpool Weekly News* apart – the coverage averaged less than 3 per cent of all public service news. The two services seem virtually nil category so far as the Liverpool dailies are concerned, though, yet again, they exemplify the *Liverpool Weekly News*'s social concern. As before, too the *Wallasey News* and *Birkenhead News* show similarities in the levels both of public demands reported and the supportive attitudes of the papers. While neither service would want any detailed case publicity – for obvious social reasons – it might have been expected that both would at least be given occasional and perhaps larger background information pieces – that in short, the *Liverpool Weekly News* and *Birkenhead News* levels would be more typical. Moreover, it is generally acknowledged that a central problem in the provision of social welfare is that many people do not know their welfare rights or how to use the services provided. These local papers were clearly of little help.

This sample of amply, moderately and little covered services reveals how much the coverage of services varies in volume and kind between newspapers. They clearly have different patterns of coverage in different areas of service – a newspaper taking a lead, or permitting itself to be used as a vehicle for some political activity in one area of service will not necessarily do so in another area. The position of the *Liverpool Weekly News* is clearly different from that of the other papers. The *volume* of its coverage as a proportion of the whole is not, perhaps, significantly different from the other weeklies, but it is different in *kind*. There are fewer single 'mentions' and a rather higher proportionate use of large features. But the main distinctive feature is that the paper sees itself as a forceful tribune of the people. It is self-consciously 'democratic' in an older, nineteenth-century populistic sense. This goes further than simply allowing its letter column to be open for readers to ventilate grievances, though this is clearly a major policy. It is more that its style is to present political news and comment in terms of conflict and disclosure, of council sins of omission or commission. All newspaper reporting has this element, but no other paper on Merseyside at least, makes it its main political style. The *Liverpool Weekly News*'s tone is that of the crusading, waspish 'outsider', whereas the other papers give the impression of being 'responsible', of being fairly close in tone and sympathy to the local leaders.

Despite the differences between newspaper coverage of local authority services there is, nevertheless, a discernible rank order of coverage. Table 9 distinguishes three broad groups of services. The first, those that habitually receive on average over 11 per cent of the total, comprises education, housing and planning. The second, whose coverage ranges between 7 and 10 per cent (and is capable in some papers of entering the first group – transport in the *Wallasey News* being the obvious example) includes highways, police and transport. The final group is of services receiving little coverage and comprises welfare, health, children, finance, parks and gardens, baths, libraries, cleansing and fire and ambulance. Attention to some of these, e.g. libraries and baths, was minimal, while others, e.g. fire and ambulance, maintained a coverage of a steady 3–4 per cent.

This rank order must be the result of the accumulated effect of the nature of these services, the *new* information they generate week by week, and their general relevance as perceived by the bulk of readers; and journalistic perceptions of these.

Table 9. *Local government services – rank order of coverage and coverage groups*

|  | L.W.N. | | L.D.P. & L.E. | | W.N. | | B.T.H. | | B.N. | |
|---|---|---|---|---|---|---|---|---|---|---|
|  | Rank | % | Rank | % | Rank | % | Rank | % | Rank | % |
| Education | 2 | 18·3 | 6 | 7·6 | 2 | 16·8 | 1 | 24·6 | 1 | 18·1 |
| Housing | 1 | 30·6 | 2 | 15·6 | 5 | 8·5 | 2 | 15·2 | 6 | 9·8 |
| Planning | 3 | 10·2 | 1 | 16·3 | 3 | 11·6 | 3 | 12·8 | 2 | 16·3 |
| Highways | 4 | 9·9 | 3 | 14·6 | 5 | 8·5 | 5 | 7·6 | 3 | 14·0 |
| Welfare | 5 | 5·4 | 13 | 1·4 | 10 | 2·6 | 10 | 2·6 | 13 | 1·4 |
| Police | 6 | 4·3 | 4 | 11·1 | 4 | 8·6 | 4 | 10·7 | 5 | 11·4 |
| Children | 6 | 4·3 | 14 | 0·3 | 14 | 0·5 | 13 | 1·1 | 13 | 1·4 |
| Parks | 7 | 3·2 | 14 | 0·3 | 8 | 4·3 | 11 | 2·4 | 12 | 1·6 |
| Transport | 8 | 2·7 | 5 | 10·8 | 1 | 18·2 | 12 | 2·3 | 4 | 12·0 |
| Health | 8 | 2·7 | 9 | 3·5 | 7 | 6·4 | 6 | 6·0 | 7 | 3·7 |
| Fire/ ambulance | 9 | 2·1 | 8 | 5·2 | 9 | 3·2 | 9 | 3·4 | 8 | 3·3 |
| Finance | 11 | 1·1 | 7 | 3·9 | 6 | 7·3 | 7 | 4·0 | 9 | 3·0 |
| Library | 12 | 0·5 | 10 | 2·8 | 11 | 1·4 | 8 | 3·6 | 11 | 1·7 |
| Cleansing | 13 | 0·2 | 11 | 2·4 | 12 | 1·3 | 14 | 1·0 | 10 | 1·8 |
| Baths | 10 | 1·6 | 12 | 2·1 | 13 | 0·7 | 10 | 2·6 | 14 | 0·4 |

| *First Division* | *Second division* | *Third division* | |
|---|---|---|---|
| 11% + | 7–10% | Under 7% | |
| Education | Highways | Welfare | Baths |
| Housing | Police | Health | Libraries |
| Planning | Transport | Children | Cleansing |
|  |  | Finance | Fire/ambulance |
|  |  | Parks/gardens | |

Thus far the discussion has centred around the total number of mentions. It is reasonable to assume that small items are not, on the whole, regarded as 'important news' either by journalists or by readers. Many are merely 'fillers'. What proportion of newspaper mentions are large and what proportion are small items? This is of particular importance in the coverage of current 'news' for this is likely to dominate the front page. An examination of this question for four of the largest services is revealing (Table 10). In these services the preponderance of news items is very clearly of the small 'filler' kind. The *Wallasey News* in particular relies heavily on these, e.g. there are eight times more 'snippets' about the police than items of substance, and six times more such items in the area of planning. There is still a preponderance of small items in the realm of reported public demands, but the papers' readiness to give demands prominence in 'large' items is also clear. For example,

Table 10. *Ratio of large to small mentions*

| | Education | | Housing | | Planning | | Police | |
|---|---|---|---|---|---|---|---|---|
| | A.I | B.I | A.I | B.I | A.I | B.I | A.I | B.I |
| | L S | L S | L S | L S | L S | L S | L S | L S |
| *Bootle Times Herald* | 1:1·5 | 1:1·7 | 1:0·6 | 1:1·1 | 1:0·58 | 1:1 | 1:0·62 | 1:2·7 |
| *Birkenhead News* | 1:1 | 1:2·4 | 1:1·1 | 1:2·3 | 1:1·2 | 1:1·8 | 1:0·57 | 1:4·5 |
| *Wallasey News* | 1:1·4 | 1:1·8 | 1:1·5 | 1:3·3 | 1:2·5 | 1:5·9 | 1:1·75 | 1:8 |
| *Liverpool Daily Post* and *Liverpool Echo* | 1:1 | 1:1·8 | 1:1 | 1:1·4 | 1:0·62 | 1:1·7 | 1:2 | 1:0·81 |
| *Liverpool Weekly News* | 1:0·17 | 1:1 | 1:0·40 | 1:1 | 1:0·5 | 1:0·5 | 1:2 | 0:0·3 |

L = Large    S = Small

the *Liverpool Weekly News* on education and the *Bootle Times Herald* on housing and planning are clear cases. Since the 'large' category excludes most readers' letters, then the majority of the large items are either front page items or prominently displayed on news pages. The newspapers, in short, do not bury the demands they print. The demand of a councillor or other spokesman *is* likely to make the front page.

How often does political news appear? Some indication of this can be given in two ways. First, by dividing the grand total of mentions by the number of issues; for the weeklies, it is found that the *Liverpool Weekly News* and the *Bootle Times Herald* average five per issue, the *Wallasey News* seven mentions. For the *Birkenhead News* – a bi-weekly – its weekly average is a product of two issues and comes to just over five mentions. The average of course, must be seen against the nearly two dozen service and other areas of coverage. News, of course, bunches up and does not appear – however defined – in neat, weekly items; the reader's memory is relied on to provide the connections, the cross-references, the awareness of 'what' is going on. While it is clear that headlining and front-paging are factors in estimating the impact of coverage, it is nevertheless salutary to see this in the context of the small *total* of items that tend to appear in any one issue.

The point is reinforced if, secondly, the year by year distribution of mentions of services in each paper is examined. Only the Birkenhead, Bootle and Wallasey papers were totally read for this purpose and Table 11 presents the findings for four important services.

All four services chosen have a mix of types of coverage. Education and transport were chosen because both were a source of controversy, while housing and police were taken as examples of high fairly routine coverage. In education we can see the impact on coverage of the comprehensive education question which reached a peak in the early 1960s, declined, and then revived again after 1968. In transport we can see the impact of timetable reorganisation, leading to protests against reduced services, and also of strikes in the period after 1966. Housing and police totals vary, over the years, there being no single underlying cause, police amalgamations and the progress of large council housing schemes being only two of very many topics of recurring interest. What is clear is that even in services with high news value, coverage is by no means weekly.

At the end of this period the Bootle and Wallasey papers went over to web-offset, and greatly improved their format. News coverage, however, continued to be bunched so that even in major services ten items over, say, three issues, would be followed by long periods of silence. In the smaller news areas the normal coverage was silence punctuated by tiny groups of items. Local political news was often the lead story but it tended to be a leader with few followers in any one issue.

### CONCLUSION

Newspapers are profit-making business organisations supplying information and diversion to their readers. In the six studied, nearly half the total space is devoted to commercial information of various kinds, the revenue from which allows the newspaper to continue publication. Judged by this continuance we may assume that as purveyors of commercial information they are an effective means of communication. The rest of the space is given over to regular

Table 11. *Year by year selected service coverage (mentions) (three newspapers)*

| | Education | | | Transport | | | Housing | | | Police | | |
|---|---|---|---|---|---|---|---|---|---|---|---|---|
| | B.N. | B.T.H. | W.N. | B.N. | B.T.H. | W.N. | B.N. | B.T.H. | W.N. | B.N. | B.T.H. | W.N. |
| 1962 | 21 | 18 | 37 | 17 | 1 | 60 | 26 | 9 | 26 | 21 | 17 | 20 |
| 1963 | 23 | 24 | 64 | 22 | 2 | 33 | 32 | 29 | 16 | 15 | 18 | 26 |
| 1964 | 22 | 41 | 80 | 7 | 2 | 39 | 8 | 24 | 22 | 15 | 14 | 22 |
| 1965 | 63 | 48 | 25 | 41 | 3 | 30 | 28 | 50 | 9 | 40 | 13 | 23 |
| 1966 | 67 | 45 | 38 | 24 | 3 | 34 | 27 | 33 | 38 | 30 | 24 | 23 |
| 1967 | 33 | 60 | 31 | 45 | 11 | 98 | 17 | 28 | 21 | 44 | 27 | 21 |
| 1968 | 85 | 81 | 40 | 54 | 12 | 29 | 29 | 42 | 28 | 49 | 34 | 16 |
| 1969 | 71 | 59 | 49 | 53 | 1 | 57 | 40 | 15 | 37 | 24 | 14 | 17 |
| Average | 46·8 | 49·3 | 45·0 | 32·8 | 4·2 | 48·7 | 25·8 | 28·7 | 24·6 | 29·7 | 20·1 | 21·0 |

features of interest to particular readers – women, children – and to general news of all kinds – social, political, sporting, personal. Thus political news faces considerable competition for space in the paper and, also, for the reader's *attention*. The attempt to judge the effectiveness of the paper as a means of political communication is thus much more difficult.

News of local government and politics is clearly a staple for local newspapers. Excluding the holiday period of July and August, political news of some kind almost always appears somewhere on the front page of the average issue of the weekly; and, not infrequently, forms the lead story. But politics or 'local government' stand for a dozen and a half areas of public service and at least half a dozen other areas of interest – civic events, the Mayor, the Town Clerk, news of political parties, local M.P.s and a little news of these from adjacent districts. For the journalist on the local *daily* paper, moreover, there is the much wider range of localities, and the national news, to be remembered. Together, both considerations absorb much of the extra space he disposes of when compared with the weekly journalist. Thus, while the total volume of local political news in relation to other news is often quite large, its nature seems predestined to be highly fragmented, demanding from the reader a large measure of background knowledge to make it intelligible. The possibility of relative infrequency of news in any one service area reinforces this unsatisfactory situation.

The consequences are very clear in the papers we have examined. Apart from a front page 'splash' on a current controversy, local politics generally appears in the form of snippets, spread over all the news pages. Some areas of public service hardly ever get a mention and others do so only as they fit in with journalistic preconceptions of news value. The parks service, for example, rates few items, the largest of which is usually the almost mandatory picture of the first flowers of spring being enjoyed by the nearest available pretty secretary. Other services are often covered tangentially to some eruption in council or committee, the reporting of which is likely to be highly personalised. Little wonder, therefore, that perceptions of local government activity are idiosyncratic and fragmented. Even when – as in the case of the *Liverpool Weekly News* – the paper is predisposed to vent demands on local government, the coverage of these is sporadic and provides little background information for the reader. The papers do not intervene editorially to a very great extent, or in any strong consistent direction, and, especially in the weeklies, the process of editorialising often lags behind the coverage, so that, at times, a reader may have to work hard to recall what is currently being 'thundered' about.

We have observed here some significant features of the kind of political news coverage provided by local newspapers. The *Liverpool Weekly News* marked itself off by its readiness to be a vehicle for the presentation of individual and group demands upon local government. For the rest, some differences must be attributed to the different performances and problems of local authorities, on the one hand, and popular reactions to them, on the other. Above this, we must attribute some variation between the levels of reported demands to editorial choice and the resources of the paper. This choice is most apparent with respect to the paper's own attitude to making demands on, or offering supports to, the local administration. Thus the dailies were noticeably higher on demand stimulation than the three borough weeklies, and noticeably better in providing background information on services. Conversely, the borough weeklies were noticeably more supportive of their local government than the Liverpool papers, a disposition which coincides with their greater attention to covering political news other than of local services – that is civic and party news, especially in their emphasis on the former.

The kind of news thus presented, then, differs, sometimes very significantly from paper to paper. They all tend, however, to share a certain manner of presentation. There is a heavy reliance on snippets, and major news items about local government usually relate to a specific controversy on the council which is then reported 'raw' with comparatively little informational or interpretative assistance to the reader. The reader is thus offered a mélange of items which may afford him some diversion, some sense of being 'in the know', but may also, and just as easily, create in him a sense of local government being bewildering and dull.

The heart of the matter is in what the newspapers actually say. It is here that they reveal, not only their towns, but themselves. Analytical methods have uncovered the outlines of differing attitudes and preoccupations both of the towns and the journalists. Now we must make these dry bones live.

# 6

# What the papers said: case histories

INTRODUCTION

Our aim in this chapter is to examine the manner of newspaper coverage of selected issues to see how they reveal themselves in their attitudes toward their communities. The issues chosen differ slightly between the papers and some attention is given to news areas unique to one or other of the boroughs. In this way we hope to show something of the newspapers' political style in the 1960s. We also examine the treatment given by all the papers to one event which impinged, or promised to impinge, on the whole conurbation, namely the proposals for local government reorganisation contained in the Redcliffe–Maud Commission Report of June 1969. The character of the newspapers is thus caught in the 'moving picture' of their separate treatment of several news areas and what turned out to be the 'still shot' of their treatment of a common, simultaneously perceived area of news of potentially great local significance. Throughout, it is possible to discern a common thread of political belief; belief in the 'good of the town' as the highest value, against which criterion all political action ought to be judged. This leitmotif will recur throughout the ensuing discussion.

First then, the weeklies, beginning with the three outer borough newspapers – the *Wallasey News* and the *Birkenhead News*, and the *Bootle Times Herald* – then the *Liverpool Weekly News*, and finally the two dailies, the *Liverpool Daily Post* and the *Liverpool Echo*.

## THE THREE BOROUGH WEEKLIES

The *Birkenhead News* saw political life in the town in fairly uncomplicated terms. It supported whatever Town Hall was doing, and gave a favourable interpretation of its policies. This was so even where the 'man in the street' might be presumed to think otherwise. It regretted and tried to damp down controversy. But where, as in education, controversy was unavoidable, it found itself in accord with the Conservative Party's views. While it 'took an interest' in certain town problems, it could not, with a few exceptions, be said to have championed any major cause, or lent its columns to others to champion. Throughout the period, the Labour Party was the majority party on the council, its tenure partly prolonged by anachronistic ward boundaries. It was, therefore, very much part of the town's 'establishment'. Neither the Labour-dominated administration nor the Conservative minority appear to have given the paper much cause to depart from its general 'establishment' stance.

The paper's typical response to a situation was to encourage sympathetic understanding of the Town Hall point of view. It accepted that the latter worked for the 'good of the town', usually defined in terms of commercial progress, which was worth sacrifice. On 5 January 1966 an editorial dealt with housing needs. It explained that planning and development schemes were affecting the Housing Committee's capacity to meet general housing needs. Tunnel approach-road building alone would require the earmarking, for rehousing of displaced residents, of 30 out of every 100 new houses, while only 15 out of 100 would be available for general housing needs. However,

Central redevelopment, which has also meant much housing demolition . . . is designed to increase Birkenhead's importance as a shopping centre and is also being given priority by the council. With a considerably increased need for housing, the Housing Committee in the immediate future will be severely restricted in meeting general housing needs. Birkenhead's progress inevitably means hardship for some townspeople.

At no point, then or earlier, was this choice of priorities questioned, nor was it ever considered whether there was any real need for 'central redevelopment', i.e. a large new shopping centre alongside one where many of the multiple stores were already represented, and only two miles from a shopping centre of regional importance. Again, the paper's response to the conclusion of negotiations with other boroughs over the new Mersey tunnel was that Town Hall had done its best and the people should be duly thankful.

The ratepayers should be grateful to those who were responsible for negotiating this successful outcome to what at one time seemed an impasse and there should be no dissenting voices at tonight's electors' meeting.

74

Editorial comment on transport was equally sympathetic. On 21 April 1965 the paper commented on an all-round increase in bus fares.

The management has big difficulties in manning all its services. For all that, the Municipal Transport Department has an impressive record of efficiency, and clearly it accepts all its problems as a challenge.

Again on 27 July 1966, the paper had to report reductions in the town's transport service. On this occasion the paper argued for subsidising the service out of the rates, and that cost consciousness could not be the only consideration. The editorial, however, concluded lamely

It will be generally agreed that many difficulties and problems have to be faced in the running of the department and it is appreciated that the committee are doing their best to cope with them.

One of the problems had been alluded to on 15 January 1966 – the absenteeism or lateness for work of bus crews, which one morning ran at 18 per cent.

The difficulties of the department are seriously aggravated by the attitude of too many employees who appear to want to fix their own working hours.

As elsewhere the comprehensive education question was for a time a prominent concern of the town and the paper. In contrast with, for example, Wallasey, the Birkenhead paper itself weighed in heavily in the controversy. Clearly, here was a case where, for once, there was a clear party division, and where the self-evident 'good of the town' appeared under attack by the majority party on the council. There are no doubt many factors which explain the difference in attitude of the Birkenhead and Wallasey papers on this issue, but it is probably significant that the Conservative Party was the one in control in Wallasey and was responsible for initiating a comprehensive scheme, whereas in Birkenhead they were in a minority, unambiguously committed to the defence of the town's direct grant schools.

At first, the paper's attitude to the issue was entirely characteristic of its line on the town's politics in general. On 23 January 1965, there was a feature article, unsigned, on school reorganisation. It gave background information and included details of the town's

direct grant schools and outlined the specific problems of the
Roman Catholic schools. At all costs, controversy was bad and
must be avoided:

> Birkenhead Education Committee has across the years won a reputation
> for progressiveness and high standards. That is a reputation it seeks
> jealously to guard.
>   At the same time its policy now is reorganisation. The dangers of
> fierce controversies are obvious. The Education Committee have a right
> to hope that their proposals, when they are revealed, will be examined
> with goodwill and that parents and others vitally involved will expect
> that there will be no rigidity of action by the Committee . . .
>   Presumably the Education Committee have been anxious that the
> consultations that have been going on should not be prejudiced by con-
> troversy and there is reason to believe they have been successful.

A fortnight later, on 3 February, an editorial entitled 'Making up
their Minds' outlined the alternatives before the sub-committee on
reorganisation. It expected they would go for the adaptation of
existing institutions. 'It retains schools of which present and past
pupils are proud', while abolishing the eleven-plus. The editorial
thought 'it could be that secondary school reorganisation in the
town will not be so violently controversial as some have feared'.

So far, the paper did not spell out the reasons for its abhorrence
of controversy. Like so much else, it was presumably considered
self-evident. Eighteen months later, alarm had become manifest. In
July 1966 the paper reported an Education Committee meeting
in which it was made evident that the committee would not, in the
long term, be requiring places in the direct grant schools. On the
27th the paper obtained a statement from the chairman of the
governors of Birkenhead School, saying that this was a challenge
to the school's future, but one which they did not fear, etc., etc.
There was an accompanying editorial entitled 'Cause for Concern',
in which the concern was that schools like Birkenhead School, in
existence for over 100 years, might not be able to carry on.

> The hope will be that in any future plan the direct grant schools will
> be able to continue to provide the bright threads that have for years
> added lustre to the educational pattern in the town . . .
>   There are many people in Birkenhead who, whilst agreeing with the
> general principle of comprehensive education, do not approve of the
> way it is proposed to introduce it here, and a safeguard for the direct
> grant schools, rather than a threat to their survival, is one of the provi-
> sions which would be welcomed.

On 3 August the paper became even more explicit, and understandably so, for the emotions of the town's establishment (except, in this case, for the Labour Party leaders) were clearly much engaged by the problem of the school's future. In this issue the paper's elder statesman, Wrayford Willmer, who was given to penning articles of magisterial timbre from time to time, weighed in with a piece on Birkenhead School. He praised the activities of the sports teachers and cadet corps in 'teaching young people the meaning of life and the problems that they are likely to meet'. It was much better, he said, to build on the legacy of the past than to start afresh from the beginning. He did not believe the people of the town realised 'what is afoot' with regard to the direct grant schools and Birkenhead School in particular. 'I am quite sure that most of them would not want to risk destroying a going concern of such obvious benefit to the town and the country . . .'

Ward boundaries was another issue on which the paper had strong views, and once again the interest of the town as a whole demonstrably coincided with that of the under-represented Conservative Party. The paper's interest may of course, have arisen from a desire to see 'fair play', but readers might be sceptical, in view of the *News*'s tendency to discuss future electoral prospects in the town in terms of the fortunes of the Conservative Party. For example, on 28 April 1965 an editorial discussed Conservative hopes. 'Efficient ward organisation . . . is vital . . . Hopes of Conservative gains are slim.' In January 1966 the Tories were presented with a challenge to make the town's Bebington and Egerton wards 'as vigorously Conservative as they once were'. On 2 October of the previous year the editorial had expressed sympathy for the Conservatives from Birkenhead who had had to cross a constituency boundary in order to be addressed by the Conservative M.P. for Bebington (Mr Howe) and had had to resolve their difficulty over the proprieties by meeting in a private house. On 20 October the editorial strongly supported Mr Howe, in his efforts to give the Home Secretary powers to adjust local boundaries where local authorities were unwilling to do so. 'It is not', said the paper, 'a matter of politics to say that boundary revisions are urgent.' This revealed a strange forgetfulness of the fact that only three weeks earlier the paper had editorialised on the party political implications of the present ward boundaries.

The paper gave space to M.P.s and parliamentary candidates to write on a variety of subjects. On 26 April 1965 it carried an article on housing problems by the prospective Labour candidate for Bebington, 'who in this article expresses his personal views'. Such a qualification was often omitted in the case of Conservative candidates and M.P.s.

Demands arising from the populace which might run contrary to the 'good of the town' syndrome were reported but almost never received editorial comment. In July 1969 a small-shopkeepers' spokesman complained bitterly that the town's planners were channelling all shopping into the central area and giving the shop-keepers who were forced to close very poor compensation. He said

This town deserves no other name than 'by-pass Backwater'. And it is the town hall officials and town councillors who have made Birkenhead one of the shabbiest nonentities in the north west. [23 July]

Another of the town's problems was highlighted in the same month when a group of squatters took over an empty house (18 July) and the paper carried several related items. But neither on this nor on the plight of the small shopkeepers was there any editorial comment. Instead, the paper was editorialising (18 July) on 'The pride that the people of Birkenhead take in their new fly-over system'. The flyover, however, was 'good' news for the town. Homeless people and ruined shopkeepers were not. And the *Birkenhead News* was committed to 'good' news, otherwise it would hardly have printed on the front page of its next issue, 25 July 1969, a reader's letter saying how much the national dailies depress her, until she picks up the *Birkenhead News* and sees

Schoolchildren, saying 'thank you' to a loved cleaner; Boy Scouts help-ing 'Birkenhead Spring Clean' collecting rubbish; council tenants gain-ing permission to paint houses, brightening otherwise drab streets; Mr Lloyd on his £1,000 charity walk etc. etc. On the front page, scarcely one depressing item of news. Good news, inspiring news. And TRUE – quite as true as the bad news . . . which, of course, has to be reported . . . And may the Birkenhead News continue to give inspiring news on its FRONT PAGE.

The *Wallasey News*'s attitude to political life was perhaps the most complex of the three outer borough papers. Far from being con-cerned to keep controversy in the town down to a minimum, for 'the good of the town', the *Wallasey News* lent itself to controversialists and campaigners on numerous occasions during the 1960s. On its own account it took no very clear party line. It did support, generally, and, on occasions, vigorously, what might reasonably be considered to be the views of the man in the street – or in the case of Wallasey, man on the bus and ferry. There were important issues on which it took no line at all – such as the Redcliffe–Maud report. Although no obvious party bias was evident, it showed, at the least, distaste for the vigorous polemical style adopted by the Labour party; and gave somewhat more prominence to the views of the Liberal leader than his party, on grounds of numerical strength, might have expected.

The comprehensive education controversy in 1964–5 was, next to transport, the most acerbic issue in Wallasey in the 1960s. A very striking feature of this controversy was the degree to which the protagonists used the letter columns of the paper to put their views before the public. For example, Councillor Gershman, Labour spokesman on education, published (on 25 July and 8 August 1964) two successive 'letters' on Labour's educational principles and reasons for pressing the comprehensive issue. The first was roughly 18 column-inches long, the second 36 column-inches. On 15 August he followed this with a letter two full columns long entitled 'Why Labour Wants the 11 Plus Abolished'. A reply came on 19 September with one and a half columns from Mr Oliver, chairman of the committee of grammar schools opposing comprehensivisation. On each of the two following weeks, 26 September and 3 October, Messrs Gershman and Oliver took, between them, a complete page, less advertisements and a few weddings.

At no time during this correspondence did the paper give its own opinions on education, relying in its editorials on uncontroversial statements on such comparatively bland topics as the expansion of the town hall, a civic theatre, and the road building programme. The controversy had, however, a concrete focal point in the special meeting of the Education Committee held at the end of September. Beyond giving space to the controversialists the paper did nothing to herald this event. The meeting itself was reported on 3 October in two columns of two-thirds of a page, under the headline 'The Uncomprehensiveness of it all'. The report was spiced with some reportage at the beginning –

They had expected to 'get cracking'. In fact they got almost nowhere. The committee adjourned on Tuesday after a four hour sitting in which they took no decision of any kind – except that the teacher's views be invited and that they should meet again. Old points and prejudices were given a new airing. It was argumentatively the mixture as before . . . The committee were required by a council directive to submit a plan by November 19th. It seems unlikely they will meet the deadline.

The issue remained very much alive in the next issue, on 10 October. The second front page story dealt with an 'angry Labour attack' on the (Conservative) education committee chairman, by the leader of the Labour Party, who accused the chairman of delaying tactics, and of failing to guide the committee along the lines laid down by the council. The Labour leader said that unless the council changed the Education Committee the town would still have the eleven-plus until the Government stepped in and said it must go. A move against the chairman, however, was 'soundly defeated', several members expressing 'disgust and regret at such a move'. The paper itself was at long last stung into making its own comment, still not on the substantive issue at stake but about the Labour Party's abrasive political style.

In a way one must admire the zeal and unflagging energy with which the Labour group on the Town Council, under Mr. Bill Wells, sticks to the motto it has adopted from a famous statesman that the duty of an opposition is to oppose. But even if one accepts the dictum are they not carrying it too far? . . . A town council is not a parliament. It is imperative for the smooth running of the town's affairs that the day to day business of the corporation should not be held up unavoidably, and that regard should be had for those who have to see that business is properly attended to.

The editorial went on to explain Labour's concern to keep itself free from all entanglements and bargains, an attitude which it found

understandable in a virile party jealous of its integrity, but we think they have nothing to fear by being less dogged . . .

Those whose duty it is to report the Town Council meetings describe many of the debates as time wasting, repetitious, exhausting the patience of many members and onerous to anxious officials whose work both at the Council meetings and at their desks is made burdensome.

It would be a relief if the appeal recently published in the *News* for a greater measure of goodwill among all the parties on the Council received the attention it deserved.

This appeal had been published on 26 September. In it a Liberal alderman had called for a 'goodwill conference' of the party leaders to explore ways of speeding up council meetings so as to reduce the need for special meetings to deal with business held over from the normal programme of meetings. He alleged that the Labour group were bringing the town's affairs to a standstill. The Labour leader, asked by the *News* to comment, had said 'our job is to oppose in a reasonable way' and 'the electorate would judge by their criteria' and not 'by the comments of one Alderman who runs squealing to the press when he can't get his own way in a private meeting of a top committee in the town hall'.

In choosing to make its stand on the issue of the manner of conducting the town's business rather than the substantive content of that business the paper adopted a stance tempting, no doubt, to all local papers when faced with an issue that was both highly complex and highly controversial. It made a strongly worded contribution which could be construed as discharging its responsibilities as a leader of public opinion, while actually evading the central issue at conflict. Exasperation with the political style adopted by the main opposition party might well have been justified. In any event, the paper, knowing the easy dividends to be gained by presenting this as a case of 'politicians versus the good of the town' discerned it as the easiest of all political wickets on which to bat.

Meanwhile the paper continued to give large areas of letter space to the leading educational controversialists. The same issue, 10 October, contained another full page, less advertisements and one wedding, of letters, mostly 'Personal Replies' of over 12 column-inches.

Although featuring in every issue except one since July, the battle over education achieved lead item on the front page only on 31 October. This was headed 'Move to Salvage the Grammar Schools' and gave an account of a plan by the Ratepayers' Association, with comments from a Ratepayers' councillor and the Labour leader. The editorial, as usual, was on another matter, though not a trivial one – the annual report of the Medical Officer of Health. On 7 November was unveiled the 'Hutty plan' for 'guided parental choice at 13' which the Education Committee chairman, Mr Fred Hutty, was to put to the council on the 19th. In addition to the news story there was a report by the Director of Education on how the scheme would work. For once the editorial was also on the same theme. Since a definitive plan had been brought out, the *News* was prepared to back it. Under the heading 'Hard homework on the 11-plus', the paper said

It sounds interesting. It seems workable. It holds out the promise of new benefits and would seem to retain the best aspects of the system now operating. If there is to be radical change, something along the lines it suggests would seem worth thorough examination. That, we hope, is what it will get . . . Probably there is no such thing as a perfect solution. It is an idea supported by practicability and a good measure of common sense.

As far as reportage was concerned, the unveiling of the plan was the climax. The actual adoption took place two weeks later. The paper, as always, continued to open its letter columns to controversial opinion, including the opposition of the teachers through the National Union of Teachers' working party, who regarded the Hutty plan as the 'least satisfactory' of those proposed. The reportage on 21 November of the actual decision to adopt the plan, with a Liberal–Labour amendment, was given a relatively brief space at the bottom of the front page. A competitor in the newsworthiness stakes had emerged in the form of a council decision, seemingly coming out of the blue, to scrap the New Brighton to Liverpool ferry service. This decision and its consequences, the offer of the New Brighton Tower Company to run the ferries instead, the activities of a New Brighton Defence Committee and the circulation of a petition, swamped the attention which might otherwise have been given to the apparent consummation (not, as it later turned out, the final one) of the comprehensive issue. It rumbled on in the letter columns; and there was something of a ripple caused by the resignation speech of the headmaster of the Grammar School (and one of the leading epistolaries), who, according to the Mayor, had cast aspersions on the authority of the Council.

Clearly, the paper was unhappy in dealing with the education issue. It was too divisive, and the paper dared not take sides. It was too complicated, and the paper lacked the expertise to judge between arguments. And in Galtung's terms, it unfolded on the wrong 'frequency' so far as the paper was concerned.

By contrast, the threatened ferry closure was ideal news, and accordingly it got, on 21 and 28 November, the largest leading items for this whole period, with an editorial ('Should snap vote decide ferry's fate?') on the latter date. Like the education issue, it could be classed as one of the few of community-wide concern. But unlike it, it was short and sharp in its impact and was clear cut in its implications for the way of life of thousands of readers.

The attitude of the man in the street was likely to be unambiguous and could be backed with few qualms. It was less obviously a 'party issue'. It was one where the 'good of the town' seemed to point clearly in one direction – against the closing of this link. Perhaps most important of all, the popular appeal of the ferry's future as a political issue indicated the extent to which the education issue appeared to be a conflict among an élite of education experts and party ideologues, conducted in a rarefied atmosphere away above most people's heads. The space the paper gave to lengthy and detailed letters on the subject probably reinforced this impression rather than enlightened the public. There was a clear need here for the paper to assume the job of interpreter, which is signally failed to do.

The problems of the ferry services, and of the town's bus services, were a constant source of newsworthy material during the 1960s. Because of the geography of the town, these were even more vital than elsewhere, and more acutely difficult to run. The town was gripped in what seemed like a vicious circle of cuts in services, rises in fares, shortages of revenue. Bitter conflict arose on several occasions. Transport could be said to be the one issue on which, regardless of the party in power (Conservative for most of the period), the paper attempted both to lead the public in a fight against the policies of Town Hall, and at the same time to educate it in the realities of the situation. As in the case of education, the paper was notable in the use made of it by letter writers. In one issue, 8 August 1964, there were seven letters, two of them from councillors, protesting about bus service cuts. But the paper weighed in on its own account, to oppose the council's policy of resolving financial difficulties in transport services by cutting them down. In an editorial later that month the paper argued that

Clearly it is uneconomic and inefficient for passenger services to continue to be operated by individual authorities. Bold and drastic changes must come. Unified transport in the area is inevitable.

This was good prophecy, in view of the subsequent establishment of the Passenger Transport Authority for Merseyside as a whole.

In 1969, the future of the ferry services was as much in doubt as ever. On 1 August the *News* announced a rise in fares from 9*d* to 1*s*. The paper was in a crusading mood. Its main story explained that the ferries were facing a deficit of £180,000. Quotations had been obtained from the Finance Committee chairman, some Labour aldermen, and the ferry users themselves, one of whom called the 3*d* rise 'scandalous and ridiculous'. That week, the paper was not ready to editorialise, preferring to highlight its own 'Miss New Brighton' contest. On 8 August, however, it thundered

Put simply, in terms that do not beat about the bus-stop, passengers are being asked to pay out more and more for less and less. Buses have never been so few. Boats have never been run at so poor a frequency. It would seem that the council's Passenger Transport Committee learns nothing from its past mistakes. Cuts in services and jumps in fares have been tried many times. All they have done is to persuade more and more people to desert local public transport.

The use of computers and expert consultants have not, it alleged, prevented the services losing cash and customers' goodwill.

Back in 1967, when the much criticised new look bus service was dumped on rather bewildered travellers, there were certain members of the Town Council who described the 'Wallasey News' as being one-sided on the transport issue. It was even said that it whipped up public anger. What the paper said then about local transport it repeats now . . .
Anger has been with the public right from the start of the new service. It is still there. Seldom has there been anything in Wallasey on which feelings have run so high. And the new rise in fares isn't going to help ease a sorry situation.

The inequitable distribution of ward boundaries was another issue on which, when it arose, the *News* could be counted upon to hold firm opinions. The town's 'west end', consisting largely of post-war housing estates, had by the 1960s about a quarter of the total population of the town but only an eighth of the representation. Periodically the Liberal Party, who had some strength in the area, had raised the question, and received support and publicity in the *News*. An editorial on 4 July 1969, welcomed a move to redistribute representation.

The simple fact is that they are not getting a fair slice of the municipal cake . . . The position is grossly unfair, and the 'Wallasey News' has repeatedly drawn attention to it . . .

The people of the big estates

need playgrounds and parks. They need some sort of civic centre. They have had their fill of promises and let downs . . . Greater voting power in the Town Hall committee rooms could help West Enders feel that they were being brought more into line with the rest of Wallasey.

Needless to add there was a clear commercial imperative in championing this neglected but populous quarter, which housed many newcomers to the town.

This issue provides further evidence, however, of the consistent support which the paper gave to the theme of improving the quality of Wallasey's political life. It was also, as we have seen, a favourite Liberal theme. The Liberal leader returned to it in August 1965, only to be called by the Labour leader, an 'inexperienced, whiter than white, leader in charge of a tiny holier than thou group which is lost in the political wilderness'.

Certainly a notable feature of the paper was the way in which it allowed, even encouraged, party leaders to use it as a means of self-expression. Its letter columns, as we have seen, were particularly used in this way. In general the *Wallasey News*'s letter page was distinguished by serious correspondence and a comparative absence of trivial or thoughtlessly presented matter. Indeed, as often as not, the correspondents were providing more political meat than the paper itself. Front page publicity was frequently given to party leaders' views, especially those of the Liberal leader. The Liberals may have been more open to the press. Certainly their views and policies tended to receive more publicity than their numerical strength warranted, and they were generally sympathetically treated. The converse would appear to be true, in most respects, of the Labour Party.

In general the paper's stance was to hold a watching brief on behalf of its readers. Like the *Birkenhead News* it was committed to the 'good of the town', though it interpreted its duty under this in somewhat different ways. Unlike the former, the *Wallasey News* could be vigorous and combative, though not on issues that were clearly party questions. It championed the 'rules of the game', especially when it felt that party conflict threatened to disrupt them. In a town where party strife was at times intense, this was a valid and useful role, if occasionally an unadventurous one involving no risks. The paper's apparent affinity for the Liberals probably stems from the fact that their stances tended to be similar vis-à-vis the main parties.

The bulk of the paper's coverage was dictated by the output of council chamber and offices and consisted of straight verbatim reproduction. Editorials, though usually sober treatments of serious topics, only occasionally dealt with the main or even the second lead story, being almost random or capricious in their choice. At best this led to a muffling of impact. At worst it reinforced the air of being non-committal on major issues.

Finally, it should be noted that in May 1965 the council opened its committee meetings (except for the Establishments Committee) to the press and public. This had no very evident effect on reportage. In August 1965 the paper adopted web-offset, and a new layout, abandoning its presentation of large slabs of unbroken print. The move to a much brighter paper may well have had more impact on its capacity to communicate political news than any changes in its relationship with the council.


The *Bootle Times*, the *Bootle Herald*, and after their merger in 1965 the *Bootle Times Herald*, have very clearly seen the path to success as lying in the direction of the promotion and defence of Bootle. The *Times Herald* identifies with the political leadership in Bootle in so far as it seeks to revive and support local pride and 'community' and the local economy. It is, hence, of all the papers, the one most openly committed to community consensus.

Bootle has had to overcome a grim recent past and the *Bootle Times Herald* in the 1960s gave the impression at times that it had a mission to see that the town did so. The paper, in web-offset in the latter part of the period, was attractively laid out, often with coloured photographs and supplements and with a readable, engaging style. The *Bootle Times Herald* was proud of itself and proud to be Bootle's paper. Thus in December 1967 when it came second in its class – and its stable-mate the *Crosby Herald* was 'commended' – in the national Annual Newspaper Design Award Competition, the news was splashed under the headline 'A Double for *Your* Papers'. This achievement was reinforced by a steadily rising circulation. Further, success meant no change in its attitudes during the 1960s. It became, if anything, even more ready to blow its own and Bootle's trumpet now that the town had begun to change its image.

In this attitude the paper was continuing as its two predecessors had begun. In 1964 Bootle was 'twinned' with Mons in Belgium. Both the *Times* and *Herald* defended the decision to spend money on this and splashed the story in print and picture when formal ceremonies took place in June. The *Herald* emphasised that, though Bootle was basically a nineteenth-century town, it was mentioned in Domesday Book and so had a 'real history' as did Mons. Thus the headline ran 'Ancient Towns of Bootle and Mons Twinned' and their common experience in the twentieth century – great sacrifices for democracy – were stressed. Mons, like Bootle, was bravely struggling to overcome the consequences of industrialisation and, like Bootle, was being led by dedicated local leaders in the face of much difficulty. The merger of the papers reinforced this – the *Bootle Times Herald* assiduously covered any 'twinning' activity. Thus the Town Clerk was shown receiving Mons visitors, the Mons Burgomaster was photographed at the opening of the New Strand Shopping Centre and, in 1969, the paper editorialised on the value of the joint Mons–Bootle Youth Centre at Mons.

The same Bootle-boosting spirit was visible in area after area. The borough had adopted a twenty-year redevelopment plan in 1953. By the mid-1960s this was noticeably bearing fruit. In March of 1967 the Council announced that the new Bootle symbol was to be the rooster. The *Bootle Times Herald* thought this apt since the town 'has plenty to crow about'. The coverage and the announcement of further development in the Stanley Precinct was followed by an article giving an overview of redevelopment completed and in prospect. An editorial quoted with pride the Chairman of the Planning Committee commenting that Bootle *used* to be a 'figure of fun to the so-called comedians of the music halls'.

The 'new Bootle' looked to its centenary celebrations in 1968 with the *Bootle Times Herald* judiciously prodding from behind. The first meetings were held in 1967 and by January 1968 a reader was asking 'Why spend so much on such a thing?' The paper gave no direct answer, having made its ardent support clear much earlier. By May 1968 the paper front-paged growing interest under the headline 'Vast Support promised for Centenary'. There followed careful orchestration of centenary news. The borough's first woman Mayor – Alderman Bray – was succeeded by Alderman and Mrs O. Ellis who, the coverage stressed, would 'preside over the centenary'. In June, the Town Clerk, Mr Arthur Taylor, was applauded for his O.B.E.

With a great love for his home town, he had been the main driving force behind the renewal and development of Bootle, giving the town the opportunity to be one step ahead of other towns.

In the same issue a Bootle fireman was applauded for choosing to receive his Royal Life Saving Society medal in Bootle rather than in London. The departure of the Mayor and Town Clerk for Mons to coordinate the inauguration of Mons Square in Bootle and the Mons role in the centenary was extensively covered.

The Prime Minister, Mr Harold Wilson, visited Bootle in November and his remarks on opening the G.P.O. Giro were eagerly quoted.

Only half a generation ago the town was regarded as a pantomime joke. Now it is becoming a very remarkable sign of progress and change in our national life.

The actual centenary date in December consumed most of the paper, with features, news and pictures. An editorial noted how the charter had been a far-sighted move by Bootle leaders who took 'positive action in the light of a possible move northward by Liverpool'. The following week the front page was again devoted to the events this time with the stress on Mons participation.

There were to be further celebrations in the coming summer. The general satisfaction brooked no dissenting humour. When Eric Jacobs, in the *Sunday Times*, described Bootle as the 'great wild west territory' and its new housing at Netherton as 'neat, bleak and discreet', a pained editorial sharply noted how 'The town's remarkable progress and achievement has been sacrificed to a play on words.' When the June centenary celebrations came around there was large pictorial coverage of the events which were, in fact, nearly ruined by rain.

The paper found the whole affair from inception to execution much to its taste. It offered prizes for the best decorated streets, though, in passing, it might be noted that these, totalling £50, were hardly feverishly generous. Coverage *had* been generous and the paper's interest over some eighteen months was unflagging. Predictably, therefore, when the centenary was over an editorial in July 1969 asked the council to keep the various committees in being and have a two- or three-yearly festival.

The same concern with the promotion of newsworthy good things was apparent with the coverage of the abortive 'Backing Britain' campaign of early 1968 – just, in fact, as the centenary campaign was getting going. On 12 January, under the headline of 'Bootle's Been Backing Britain for Years' the story showed how quickly the campaign was spreading. The following week a leader welcomed, in unmistakable tones of local pride, the official borough blessing.

It is fitting that Bootle should have given a lead by being the first local authority to announce, officially, through the Mayor, its wholehearted support for the 'Backing Britain Campaign'.

Within a fortnight the paper's enthusiasm was mixed with mild anxiety

The *Times Herald* is keen to see that the 'Bootle Backs Britain' movement does not die an untimely death because of lack of interest or initiative. To this end any measures which firms may take in connection with the campaign will be reported in our columns.

Finally, some months later the paper wrote finis to the campaign when it covered Admiral Casper John's presentation to the Mayor of a citation recognising the sterling efforts of the borough. A town pulling itself up by its boot straps identified most easily with the national mood out of which 'Backing Britain' came.

It would be wrong, however, to suggest that the *Bootle Times Herald* was over deferential towards the party leaderships in Bootle and studiously avoided or muted controversy. As noted earlier the focus of loyalty and the concern was for Bootle as a community rather than any group of its leaders *per se*. It had its views, and in promoting them was responsible but tenacious. The borough council is not responsible for the Leeds–Liverpool canal, which is the responsibility of the British Waterways Board, but judged by the *Bootle Times Herald*'s vehemence on the danger of the canal to children, it might as well have been. The newspaper often overtly charged the British Waterways Board with negligence. Covertly the resultant pressure from highly publicised accidents was a cross for the borough council to bear – why, the paper implied, did it not confront the Waterways authority?

On housing, the paper seemed less interested in party political questions such as the sale of council houses – a real issue elsewhere – than in vandalism, dampness and litter on council estates. Here again the paper was far from deferential. It front-paged and investigated charges of dampness and shoddiness, and published tenants' complaints and letters. One such in February 1968 – during the

Backing Britain campaign – asked, from Netherton, 'If the Mayor can "Back Britain" how about her backing the tenants and helping them get their houses dry?' Twice later in the year the paper gave a lot of front page space to the alleged inadequacies of the huge Marsh Lane Estate. In January 1969 Housing Committee sensibilities were ruffled by the headline 'Rat Plague Hits Sefton Families' – Sefton was a recently finished housing estate. The tone was very clear. Bootle, a progressive showpiece community, deserved much better and the council was responsible.

Finally, education. In 1964 both *Bootle Times* and *Bootle Herald* covered Liverpool's initial steps in the comprehensive battle. The *Herald* seemed less anxious to highlight the issue, putting parental reactions in its women's gossip column. The *Times* editorialised on the implications for Bootle. The 'strongly Socialist committee will be defying certain Labour Party principles if the present system is continued with . . . [they are playing] . . . a "wait and see" game . . . while some neighbouring authorities have jumped in at the deep end.'

Two weeks later the paper carried the statement of the Deputy Chairman of the Education Committee, who noted – 'we should wait and see if there is any benefit to be gained by us from other people's mistakes'.

The question then ceased to be a first class issue as the Conservatives took over the Council. By July 1967, a consensus having emerged, the *Bootle Times Herald* hailed plans for a custom-built comprehensive school to be opened in 1969. This

will be satisfactory to many residents . . . It would seem that Bootle Education Committee are determined to produce a type of school fitted for its new role, much to be preferred than the often piecemeal effort of some other local authorities . . .

As the position of the Labour government hardened on the question, the Education Committee decided to circulate parents to ask for their views. The *Bootle Times Herald* took this to be a 'real effort on the part of the Education Committee to enlist the cooperation of parents . . .' and asked the latter to cooperate fully.

Throughout, the paper, perhaps sensing a fair measure of consensus, had sought to avoid giving the appearance of fundamental cleavage over the question. Opposing statements were not kept off the front page so much as portrayed as useful, constructive dialogue

and the battles of other authorities were made to seem unnecessary
and almost improper. Bootle would solve this problem as it solved
others. Meanwhile, it was still pioneering – in November 1967, on
the opening of a day school for especially handicapped children, the
*Bootle Times Herald* predictably headlined 'Bootle Blazes a New
Trail in Education . . .'.

The situation of the *Bootle Times Herald* was very much the
main determinant of its posture. The paper reflected the hopes and
fears of Bootle and stimulated community sentiment. If one may
infer a world view from its coverage it would be that Bootle must
cohere to survive and that for cohesion a growing local economy,
exemplary social services and civic pride and interest must be
apparent. Though operating under the umbrella of the metropolitan
dailies, the *Bootle Times Herald* could not simply fill the gaps as
does the *Liverpool Weekly News*. It has to do that *and* influence
and encourage the political leadership. In this sense the umbrella of
the dailies is irrelevant for they are not Bootle papers at all. Bootle
for them is simply a part of a much larger beat. The *Bootle Times
Herald* must then be statesmanlike and responsible for Bootle.

## THE 'LIVERPOOL WEEKLY NEWS'

The *Liverpool Weekly News* is *par excellence* a weekly paper operating beneath the umbrella and on the home ground of the two
Liverpool dailies. Quite obviously, it has been run by an editor who
believes that the dailies leave much to be desired so far as the
people of Liverpool are concerned.

The formula of the *Weekly News* seems clear enough – the paper
caters for certain popular needs and unhesitatingly makes itself a
vehicle for strident demands and opinions. Thus while the other
weeklies, and above all the *Bootle Times Herald*, are oriented
towards consensus, the *Weekly News* sees no identity of interest
between the man in the street and the 'authorities'. It is very
definitely on the side of the former, and sets out unhesitatingly to
reflect his interests both social and political. Between 1½ and 2
pages are given to reports of weddings, with a clear preference for
pictures. Again, the sporting coverage is large, racy, very local and
often front-paged. The advertising is overwhelmingly local, much
patronised by small tradesmen, smaller car-sales companies, etc.
Readers' letters often take up a whole page or more, and, as often as

not, one or two lengthy, lively, acerbic controversies rage on its pages. The focus of the paper is intensely local and the letter column is the stage on which *local* people have their say about anything and everything. Thus, alongside letters on vandalism and traffic accidents, there are often shrill exchanges on fascism, anti-Semitism, socialism, etc., all conducted in high generalities and very earnest in tone. The *Liverpool Weekly News* is nothing if not local and very lively.

It is also 'fearless' in an older tradition of journalism. Rebuked for its sensationalism by local politicians, the reply from the editor is prompt, tart and heroic. Under the heading 'Everybody's Whipping Boy' the paper's assailants were on one occasion compared to Romans beating their slaves. But

Our lords and masters should remember, however, that unlike that poor bound slave we can answer back. And despite the possibility of further assaults, we will always do so to protect the interests of all the people.

Not that the *Weekly News* regarded all journalistic activities as fair or proper. Three weeks earlier than this the paper had applauded Harold Wilson's refusal to appear on B.B.C. television – why, it asked, should he face the 'B.B.C.'s political hatchet men?'

The newspaper's attitude towards party politics and civic dignity was, then, that of the uncommitted, often puzzled yet indignant man in the street. Thus, on education and the comprehensive controversy the paper warned both against dangerous change and refusal to change at all. In an editorial – 'The Middle Cut' the paper urged

our present system is very far from being perfect and there are firm grounds for the charge that in it we had fostered a procedure that tends to throw youngsters onto the scrap heap at a ridiculously early age.

Yet, months later in 1969, the paper front-paged the arguments against the Secretary for Education's circular enjoining Local Education Authorities to proceed with comprehensive reorganisation as quickly as possible. The Secretary had clearly offended the local option preferences of the editor – and those of many of his readers. These, presumably, shared the editor's doubts on the government's priorities and initiatives. An example of these had been the editor's treatment of student unrest in the spring and summer of 1968.

In late May and early June he returned to the theme that the unrest highlighted wrong priorities – the money spent on university expansion could be much better put to work on non-university students and those in primary schools.

The editor of the *Liverpool Weekly News* was no believer in the 'permissive society', for students or anyone else. In September 1969 he was violently hostile to the squatting and occupation at 144 Piccadilly. 'It is time we withdrew our permissiveness and their permits, and made them get off and walk on their own feet, and to starve if that's what they prefer to do.'

Yet the paper was equally strident on the need for housing. In the same issue the front page story had been the potential danger to council tenants whose houses might be sold to private interests – rents, the paper had been told, might treble. A week earlier the revelations of a Shelter report had provoked in 'The Lost Ones' an indignant roar of support for immediate activity. The disclosures could be, the paper said, '. . . orchestrated to a theme of a fugue for the forlorn. A madrigal of misery in which the man who pays the landlord has also to play the tune.'

The passage may be purple, but the emotion was genuine. This style and content makes the *Liverpool Weekly News* a not unfaithful reflection of traditional working class attitudes. Local government does things *to* 'us' not *for* 'us'. Politics, anyway, is a maze or a fraud and sometimes both. Squatters and rioting students are evidence of 'progress' going wrong and maybe dangerously so. Yet, when all is said and done, life still has its milestones – funerals and marriages – and its immediate pleasures – football, racing and the current antics of the locally newsworthy. The *Liverpool Weekly News* brings a dignity to its parochial stance, which is to its credit, and brings to mind nothing less than a 'city Hampden'.

THE 'LIVERPOOL DAILY' POST AND THE 'LIVERPOOL ECHO'

Eight years of two dailies represents an enormous amount of coverage of all kinds. Arrival at a representative selection of issue areas is not easy. These are not simply *local* papers with a clearly defined readership. The orientation of the papers is regional and stress on the interdependence of city and hinterland is a strong motif. It was decided to select, bearing in mind the different kinds of *Echo/Post* readers. Thus, the establishment of the Merseyside

Passenger Transport Authority serves as an example of a regional issue having implications for large numbers of people outside Liverpool itself. Secondly, we chose an issue area which had conurban implications though a clear Liverpool focus – for this the 1968 Liverpool bus strike seemed obvious. Finally, in the comprehensive schooling question there was an area which – whatever its effects on others as an example – was domestic to Liverpool.

The announcement of the government's intention to form Passenger Transport Authorities in the conurbations under its proposed Transport Bill of 1968 came during the bus strike in Liverpool, though their thinking on this subject was, of course, known well in advance. The two events were not directly related, though the Passenger Transport Authorities were seen as an attempt to put public transport on a better long-term footing and the strike was, in part, seen as symptomatic of the need for this. The strike then, was for Liverpool journalists, a prelude to the Passenger Transport Authority.

The bus strike began on 11 March 1968 and ran on until 25 May, some eight weeks in all. The national context of the strike was the devaluation of the pound in November and the standstill on wages of December 1967. A month before the strike the city Transport Committee had decided to ask the Prices and Incomes Board to resolve an impasse created by the city busmen's wage claim – this just before the Minister had submitted the claim of all provincial busmen to the Prices and Incomes Board. Whether this independent submission was allowable was the *casus belli* by early March, the strikers arguing that the Transport Committee was anxious to use it to avoid paying.

Both papers had reported the various developments, the *Echo* more prominently than the *Post*. Once the strike began, this difference widened noticeably, the *Echo* becoming vehemently hostile very quickly. Great stress was laid on the unofficial nature of the strike. The letters column bristled with pro- and anti-strike letters. There was much coverage of miles walked to work by those unable to get lifts. A week after its outbreak the *Echo* headlined 'City Stores Recover from the Bus Strike'. In general, the line was 'the town responding heroically to privation'. Early on there had been mention of the bus strike as not Liverpool's fault, but the government's. After five weeks the *Echo* reflected local exasperation in an editorial. There were no signs that

94

authority outside Merseyside cares about the unofficial bus strike which has now cost Liverpool ratepayers, the city's trade and commerce enormous sums . . . It is scarcely conceivable that an unofficial strike of London's busmen would have dragged on for six weeks without really emphatic steps being taken from the top to end it. But Liverpool goes marching while those in the corridors of power mark time.

Three days later the Conservative leader of the council – Alderman Macdonald Steward – was front-paged as he put the blame squarely on the government in general and the Prices and Incomes Board in particular. As the two-month point was reached, so the tone became more strident. In an editorial entitled 'Why? Why?' the *Echo* argued that a productivity deal could go through and secure the public a better service and busmen greater income. Simon Fraser, the Secretary of the Trades Council had, two days earlier in the paper, attacked the Transport Department management as the stumbling block, and ended with an attack on the press, 'Why have you not reported the strike fairly? Why have you not put the blame fairly and squarely on those responsible for the management of the Transport undertaking?'

As the strike perceptibly neared its end, the *Echo* highlighted the drift of men away from employment on the buses, and this, plus the loss of passengers, became its theme thereafter. An editorial of 17 May, 'Unions and City Council' noted that 'People would like the busmen to get a square deal . . . but sympathy for them has worn very thin.' The paper continued throughout to print letters from readers who complained on behalf of other badly paid workers. One hoped that other council employees would not be forgotten as 'Many of them have not the service pay, clothing, early start pay or opportunity to work overtime as bus crews.' Even after the strike had ended, the *Echo*, unlike the *Post*, continued to highlight strike costs and passengers lost to the buses.

The chief posture of the *Echo* was that of the exasperated, outraged bus passengers compelled to walk. The city image, its economy and well-being, *demanded* an end to the strike. There was also the provincial resentment that Liverpool should be the anvil of government incomes policy, *Labour* incomes policy. The *Post*, in marked contrast, editorialised hardly at all, printed few letters and generally, while reporting hard 'news', kept its distance.

The contrast was maintained in the treatment of the Passenger Transport Authority from 1968 through to late 1969, that is, before, during and after the great bus strike. On 7 May 1968 the *Echo* front-paged the comments of Thomas Lenthall, consultant to the Massachusetts Bay Transport Authority, that United States experience did not favour Passenger Transport Authorities.

Mr Lenthall pointed out that if Merseyside now had a Passenger Transport Authority the Liverpool bus strike would have been taken up right throughout the region with all local transport services at a standstill.

In June the Minister, Richard Marsh, agreed to talks with the conurbations concerned though, as the *Echo* highlighted, 'making it clear that the Government intends to proceed with the proposal as provided for in the Transport Bill'. The summer was consumed in these discussions with the *Post* rather than the *Echo* highlighting the objections of outlying places to being included in the scheme. The *Echo*, in contrast, was frankly imperialistic for Liverpool, albeit under the guise of efficiency and good administration. An editorial of July 1968 attacked the proposed boundaries as being too constricted – 'Whitehall has yet again evinced its ignorance of where Merseysiders live and work . . . The area should be decided by railway lines.' By July 1969, with council leader Macdonald Steward as Chairman and Liverpool's Transport Manager, Albert Burrows, made Director General of the Passenger Transport Authority, Liverpool had some cause for contentment. Earlier, fears had been expressed of 'profitable' Liverpool buses subsidising deficit-ridden other services. Coming as this exercise did in the wake of bus strikes in Birkenhead and Liverpool and expectations of local government restructuring, treatment of it undoubtedly was conditioned by a heightened sense both of need and of inevitability. Within this, the non-Liverpool focus of the *Post* and the clear Liverpool focus of the *Echo* was evident.

The comprehensive controversy lasted much longer than the transport issue, if only because – given party cleavage on the question – changing party fortunes tended to lead to periodic re-examinations of the question. The change of national government in 1964 had increased pressure on local authorities to go comprehensive, and meant a hardening of Conservative attitudes, and growing concern expressed in both newspapers over the ever-increasing size of the education budgets.

The *Post*, particularly, acted as a platform for this anxiety. An editorial of January 1966 addressed itself to the £2m. increase in the education budget. Given public demand

it would be quite unreasonable to grudge the extra money . . . [The *Post* was glad to see] . . . the end of an era in which it sometimes seemed that only new buildings counted educationally . . . It is perhaps salutary to notice how small a fraction in the estimates the introduction of comprehensive schools is . . . Nevertheless the estimates do show that the activities of comparatively small pressure groups on both sides have tended to magnify this particular question at the expense of the enormous number of other educational questions which Liverpool faces.

The local elections in 1967 returned the Conservatives to power and by June 1967 a 'rethink' on comprehensive schools was announced. In July, the eleven-plus was made optional. In August the *Post* ran articles under the title of 'Politics makes perilous play with the School Plans'. The anxiety here was not so much pro-Conservative as pro-education. An article by a staff journalist commented

Political dogma is all very well in matters of foreign policy, trade unionism, budgeting – but not, emphatically not, in education . . . education is not a subject which can be approached on a doctrinaire basis – whether the doctrine is Socialist, Conservative, Liberal or what you will . . .

The posture of the two papers on this question was noticeably different. There was sufficient consensus on the need for reorganisation to prevent either from indulging in outright, ideologically motivated opposition to going comprehensive. Nevertheless the *Post*, in contrast with the *Echo*, showed greater readiness to indulge in *ex cathedra* statements on rising costs and wasteful bulding programmes. It regretted the politicisation of educational matters, a position which was Conservative in all but the capital 'C'. At times the paper appeared not to be speaking to Liverpool's problems but to the commitments and prejudices of its more middle class, non-Liverpool readership. The *Echo* – ready to pontificate on strikes and the necessity of transport reorganisation – was far less ready to come down hard on one side in this issue. Like the *Liverpool Weekly News*, it was at least aware of the problems of education for the less privileged of the city as opposed to the far suburbs, or dormitory ex-urbs. In fact, one could go further and speculate that the *Echo* was only too anxious not to align itself dangerously against many of its readership on this issue.

The six papers present somewhat different identities though all share common features. The weeklies in Birkenhead, Bootle and Wallasey clearly identify with their boroughs, sometimes posing as the only source of drive or wisdom available to them. All appear to define their chief political end as the promotion of the 'good of the town' but only occasionally were we offered even a vague definition of what this consisted of. It involved truths held to be self-evident.

Clearly it included the element of publicising worthy local institutions – e.g. sports teams, social clubs – and worthy individuals, e.g. brave firemen and policemen. Again it included the element of reinforcing community sentiment, defending the community against outside criticism and positively asserting its identity to outsiders. While this could be in the realm of sport or aesthetics it was, not surprisingly, in the realm of local government that the posture was often most clear. The papers varied in their affection for their local governors – elected and official – and their readiness to defend and enhance their reputations. In terms of its attitudes towards the activities of both council and Town Hall the *Bootle Times Herald* was the most favourable, arising from its attempt to foster a general 'Bootle consensus'; the *Birkenhead News* leaned to Town Hall but with more of a hint of deference to due authority; and the *Wallasey News* was detached, sympathetic to Town Hall's problems but, at times, equally critical, particularly of the politicians. The *Weekly News* was, of course, cool, distant, if not hostile to both politicians and administrators. It identified not with a town but a class and so was free of the burden of helping local governors with their onerous responsibilities. The daily papers, of course, were far too large and complex to be simply characterised. The *Post* exhibited a regional identity, seeing itself as a major regional voice, and was often either neutral or indifferent to specifically Liverpool problems. On occasion it sounded off with, as we noted, *ex cathedra* statements which had a distinctly conservative or middle class ring to them. The *Echo* was more the conurban paper, occasionally afraid of stepping on non-Liverpool corns. The good of Liverpool could not, for these papers, be separated from the good of the conurbation or, for that matter, the good of the Northwest.

All the papers shared the characteristic of what might be termed episodic treatment, both of the political issues and news areas we have just looked at. Whether it was on comprehensive education, transport reorganisation or whatever, the pattern was similar. A policy announcement in committee or council would be presented with some background information and some outline of the different viewpoints. The substance was too often sparse and the tone often knowingly retrospective, reflecting not what had been printed, but rather what the journalist concerned had himself been aware of. Thus the reader could be genuinely puzzled by being told that 'It has been clear for some time' when the paper had given him no such intimation. Here is evident the end-product of the operation of factors noted earlier, limited access to background information, the socialisation of journalists, the very closed nature of the local government process. All these combine to produce a situation in which important news stories seem to arise with bewildering rapidity and then disappear equally quickly. There is little attempt to inform in any systematic way or even to remind the readers that $X$ or $Y$ is pending.

Nowhere is all this more visible than in the reception of the Redcliffe–Maud Report in 1969. A proposed radical reorganisation of local government areas, with the merging of existing political entities, would have wide implications, both for the towns on Merseyside (as elsewhere) and for the journalists themselves. It is difficult to say how much a sense of community in an area depends on the existence of a separate political system. But it is at least arguable that the disappearance of separate town halls might be a prelude, in some cases, to the disappearance of separate local papers. As for the towns themselves, the report's publication would surely be a fine occasion for a 'great debate' on the merits and demerits of local self-government, conducted, if not led, by the local press.

### THE PAPERS REPORT REDCLIFFE–MAUD

The publication of the Redcliffe–Maud Report in June 1969 presents an opportunity to see how the papers reacted to a unique, once-for-all event which, unusually, hit all the towns and all the papers at the same time. It might reasonably be hypothesised that many of the indicators of the interplay between the town's political system and its newspaper would be bound up in the coverage of the Maud report. It chanced that during the same period the future of Merseyside came under scrutiny also by the publication of the long-awaited Merseyside Area Land-use and Transportation Survey (M.A.L.T.S.) in which future population and transport trends were extrapolated and alternative strategies posited. In these two events, then, the papers were presented with an opportunity to discuss the future of their areas which was without precedent since the system came into being. Both, moreover, were the products of long-established studies, rumours of the possible outcome of which had long been in circulation. In Galtung's terms, both were 'news areas' with appropriate frequency as defined by journalists, and informed treatment might reasonably be expected.

The Redcliffe–Maud Report was presented as big, important news in all the papers. They gave it front page, lead-story treatment and editorialised about its significance. To a considerable extent the weeklies relied on the *Liverpool Daily Post* and the *Liverpool Echo* and the national media to provide detailed general coverage and themselves took up local stances towards the substantive proposals. In general there was little or no preparation of the readers for the news. Equally, the coverage was brief in terms of time – a week for the dailies and single issues for the weeklies. Later in November, when the reactions of local governments were sent to the Commission, the subject had a brief revival of attention.

'Maud Splits Merseyside: threat to Democracy say Towns.' The *Post* headline of 12 June summed up the situation as the various towns of the conurbation saw it. The previous evening the *Echo* headlined 'Metropolitan Merseyside' and gave nearly 3½ full pages of detailed coverage and reactions, not only in Liverpool, but also from Birkenhead, Wallasey, Bootle and Chester. While both dailies spread themselves in lavish news and information, they differed markedly in their editorial attitudes. Declaring that the 'streamlining of local government is inevitable' but warning that the new units must be adequately financed and must not be 'remote', the *Echo* argued in favour of the proposals.

The *Post* was altogether more critical. The Prime Minister's reception of the Report was 'devious' and the Commission was wrong to see the Mersey as only a physical barrier. The Report

fails in democracy though many of the general patterns it embodies are well conceived . . . It puts administrative needs ahead of human ones . . . Bigger local authorities would destroy the sense of voluntary service which is so much a strength in smaller councils

and they would be 'largely insulated from direct public accountability at the ballot box'. Provincial councils would be even worse in this respect. While the *Echo* asked for 'more', the *Post*, with its eye on its Northwest and North Wales readership, cried 'too much'. The *Echo* also carried first reaction from the other boroughs – hostility in Chester and Bootle, wariness in Birkenhead and coolness in Wallasey.

In the days that followed, the *Echo* printed *no* letters and the *Post* one, from Birkenhead, asking 'why this obsession with regionalism?' Two other Reports received attention – both relevant to conurban problems and reform. Both papers front-paged the M.A.L.T.S. Report of 17 June – the *Echo* more welcoming for the proposed expansion of the conurbation and featuring the following day an article by Ian Craig, the municipal correspondent, on 'Chance to create a Super City'. Equally, both dailies front-paged the announcement, following the McKinsey Report on the management of the city's government, that Stanley Holmes, Liverpool's Town Clerk, was to be made Chief Executive of a reorganised administration. As with its greater coolness to Redcliffe–Maud, so with this report – the *Post* gave prominence to 'Town Hall men' worried about their jobs.

Maud may have been a brief sensation, but there was news and information about it and the daily newspapers gave a lead of sorts to public opinion.

The weeklies stand in some contrast. The *Liverpool Weekly News* gave the news a front page position the following week, but took nearly a month to editorialise and printed *no* letters in between. Although the paper had been for amalgamation of the police its attitude to Redcliffe–Maud was distinctly cool.

It can readily be seen that the grouping together of existing authorities will produce a louder voice; it is yet to be proved that it would be the voice of the people [People should tell the Minister] that they do not wish to jump out of the county council type of frying pan into the metropolitan authority fire.

Four months later, when the subject revived, the *Weekly News* was even more explicit; and with its eye on areas south of Liverpool and under Lancashire County Council it was adamant that

Had local councils, in fact, moved nearer instead of making every possible effort to get away from the grass roots, they would now have an enormous reservoir of public opinion with them in their greatest need. Instead, they have next to nothing. The public has been conditioned into apathy . . . The county councils themselves are living examples of how to remove people – the abrasive element – from local government.

The dailies' stress on necessities of large-scale government was irrelevant to the *Liverpool Weekly News*, given that large units could only compound the problem of unrepresentativeness.

In Bootle the reception was even cooler, since the identity and progressive tradition of the borough was seen to be at stake. The headline, 'We'll lose identity – Alderman', encapsulated the paper's theme and it gave little general coverage. The police merger still rankled, it seemed. Larger units were not necessarily better, as Bootle had reason to know.

An example of this right on Bootle's doorstep is the fact that Bootle rate-payers now pay more for the maintenance of a combined Liverpool–Bootle Constabulary but with no greater efficiency so far as one can gauge . . . It could well be, indeed it is to be hoped, that 'into battle' will be the cry of Bootle, whose outstanding progress and forward think-ing has long been the envy of Merseyside but which will now be in danger of being swallowed up in a gigantic soulless 'Metropolitan District'.

There was in Bootle, as elsewhere, a lull during the summer. By September the *Bootle Times Herald* was again front-paging and editorialising 'grave doubts' about Maud, and the following month hailed the twenty-seven pages of objections sent by the Council to the Commission. An editorial talked of 'municipal suicide' and asked – not rhetorically – would the housing pro-gramme be so far advanced if Bootle had not had *local* govern-ment?

Across the Mersey the report received no warmer a welcome. In Birkenhead and Wallasey the papers reflected the fears of the political leaderships for their relative autonomy and the political game as they knew it. Both papers had given occasional hints of the existence of the Redcliffe–Maud Commission during the previous years, but by and large, local government was portrayed as con-tinuing on its week-by-week existence, oblivious of the time-bomb ticking away under it. Even in the issues preceding the publication, the papers gave no preview of it. On 11 June the *Birkenhead News* led with 'M–Day; Report could bring shake-up. All change in Wirral local government?' By appearing on the actual day of the report's publication, the paper faced something of a dilemma. It had to acknowledge the importance of the event, but could only speculate on what the report might include. Hence, the lead story was the only coverage of the report. The reporter's unfamiliarity with the issue was cruelly betrayed by his spelling of 'Maude' throughout with a gratuitous final 'e'. He did, however, get the broad outline of the recommendations right, though he expected they would include community councils at the lowest level, as well as the higher tier metropolitan and provincial councils. Both papers published on 13 June, and could print a full account and appraisal of the report. But there was a considerable contrast between the treatment it got in the two papers. The *Wallasey News*'s main headline and news story was, if anything, even more than usually concerned with local minutiae – 'Firemen want apology after alderman's remarks', and the editorial, similarly, was on another matter. What coverage there was of the report bore all the marks of hasty, last minute insertion in a paper ill-geared to sudden demands of this type. On an inside page there was a bald account of the main gist of the report, while on the front page, though not in the prime position (pre-empted by the *amour propre* of the firemen), there was a column under the heading 'Leaders lash out at Maud'. The report said

Wallasey Town Council minority leaders came out strongly against this week's Redcliffe–Maud Report on local government, which would leave the borough with the same status as parish councils under the present system and no more powers.

The Labour leader was quoted as deploring the new metropolitan districts which would have 'no background to weld them together' as 'an insult to Merseysiders, while the Liberal leader, though approving the regional pattern, felt that all the functions proposed for the large second-tier authorities 'could be perfectly well carried out by Wallasey Borough Council as it is at present' and he stressed the 'personal contact between electors and elected and councillors and officers'. The leader of the council (Conservative) was less bold. 'It does not help to take up entrenched positions before the matter has been fully digested and considered . . . etc., etc.'

The *Wallasey News* clearly obtained these quotations by seeking them out. It is odd that having gone to this degree of effort, they failed to give the report greater emphasis in its placing in the paper, and failed to editorialise, however briefly. It might be argued that the late 'bursting' of Maud on the newspaper's weekly publication cycle presented it with critical difficulties. A further week's time for reflection, however, brought no evident acknowledgement of this, the paper preferring the realities of local life. The lead story was on possible rises in council rents and the editorial referred to the minister's decision to reprieve the New Brighton to Wrexham railway line. Maud was relegated to a small front page item, 'Council is to study Maud'. The council, following the cue of its leader, was to 'digest the recommendations . . . before striking any attitudes on the plan'. Clearly, the *Wallasey News* was of the same mind – so much so, in fact, that they omitted to discuss it at all. By the third issue after M-Day it had disappeared altogether.

The coverage of the *Birkenhead News* was very much fuller, and a serious attempt was made to give the report lively and comprehensive treatment. On 13 June the main headline ran 'Maud gets thumbs down' and the sub-heading 'Democracy in danger fears'. The report said that 'the death of democracy and the replacement of councillors with remote bureaucrats was forecast this week by Birkenhead's politicians and administrators . . .' Quotations had been obtained from the leaders of the three parties in the council, but also from the Town Clerk, the Clerk of Cheshire County Council, and the town's two Conservative parliamentary candidates, though not, curiously, from the (Labour) M.P.s. The quotations from the leader of the council and the Town Clerk were in thick lettering and accompanied by photographs. On an inside page there was a full page (less advertisements) on 'The Town Hall Revolution' with lengthy quotations from the report, highlighting the four faults of the present system the commissioners wanted to get rid of, with the advantages of the new system outlined. The proposals as they affected the conurbation and especially the town were selected for emphasis. An editorial asked 'Will it be better?' It expressed 'bewilderment' and wondered how much the scheme would cost, and whether it would really be more efficient. The new Metropolitan district, including Birkenhead, was 'totally artificial' and

Inevitably, there will be a feeling in Birkenhead that it will lose much of its identity in the change-over. Birkenhead has never shown any desire to be linked with Liverpool in local government and the pointer is that it will now fall under the shadow of Big Brother.

The progressive administration of the town was the equal of any 'apart from the usual criticisms which apply anywhere'. A genius for simple reaction, manifest often in past editorials, was once more revealed in the sour comment that

The commission's report says 'the present system contradicts the pattern of modern life'. In some quarters that might be regarded as an argument in favour of retention of the old system . . .

The sceptical posture was reinforced by a piece in the miscellany, 'Town Hall Beat', repeating fears of remoteness of the new representatives. The man in Higher Tranmere or Woodchurch (i.e. Mr Average Birkenhead) knows, ran the argument, that he can contact his local councillor if he wishes; but the latter will 'disappear into the maw of some monolithic structure of semi-professional local politicians'.

It was, perhaps, not the time to express doubts as to the efficacy of the present arrangements for local government in Birkenhead. But the paper's reporting surely had the effect of reinforcing the stance of 'Birkenhead *contra mundum*' which had already been adopted by the bulk of the town's political establishment. It was hard to avoid the conclusion that the paper was speaking for that establishment, taking its cue from them, rather than, despite its protestations, the man in Higher Tranmere, of whose satisfied attachment to the present system evidence was slight, one way or the other.

By curious coincidence, the 'Maud' issue included a supplement, 'Birkenhead Guide'. This was a 'survey of the town' which included an unsigned piece describing the council, the functions of its chief officers and the departments. The account was bald, institutional, unenticing.

By the next issue, 20 June, the issue of Maud was, as far as the paper was concerned, dead. As in Wallasey and Bootle, the issues of daily living in the town, perhaps more real to readers and journalists alike, surged back to the forefront. On 20 June a storm over educational provision for Roman Catholics achieved pride of place, and the parents' threat (carried out) to seek a High Court injunction, and a test case, along with an adjournment debate on the subject in the Commons, became a weekly focus of attention. More real to the town, too, was the opening, in July, of the new tunnel approach flyover scheme, again tangible evidence of a progressive administration getting on with the job.

The publication of the M.A.L.T.S. report, as well as its intrinsic interest, might have been seen as underlining the need for further discussion of the issues raised in the Maud report. In the case of the *Birkenhead News* the two were linked, though only in order to further the condemnation of them both. The editorial emphasised that it was 'a costly report' – it had cost £438,762 – a vast sum, said the editorial, even if its contents prove of great benefit. But its recommendations on transport 'do not include any startling new ideas' and meanwhile there had been 'a three year standstill in transport development while the report has been prepared'. Even if £116 millions were spent in the next decade, in 25 years from now 7,000 parking spaces would still be needed in Birkenhead centre. 'Truly the motor car has grown to dominate our lives', lamely concluded the editor. The 'Town Hall Beat' column noted that the two reports had aroused 'quite a bit of excitement' in the Town Hall, but the question remained whether the reports were really going to be put into operation or whether they were 'so much pie in the sky'.

There has rightly been strong criticism of the Maud Report, but some local councillors are not getting too hot under the collar, because they believe that the plans may never be put into operation. The dust may be allowed to settle there too.

The *Wallasey News* gave more coverage to the M.A.L.T.S. report than it did to the Maud report. Council leaders gave it, said the *News*, a 'cautious, but on the whole, warm welcome' (27 June 1969). The Liberal leader, and the chairman of the Transport Committee, were quoted.

On 4 July, the Labour candidate, and former Labour leader on the council, in a speech to the Trades Council and Labour party, under the headline 'Maud makes sense', was reported as saying that 'we should accept 95 per cent of the Maud Commission's proposals and make sure we fight the right battles over the remaining 5 per cent'. On 25 July the decision of Cheshire County Council to 'cost' the Maud plans was reported. But throughout this time the *Wallasey News* refrained from editorial comment.

The Maud report became front page news in Wallasey on one further occasion, on 27 September, when the 'vital moves in re-organisation of town' were reported, under that main headline. The suggestion (from Birkenhead) that Wallasey and Birkenhead should merge to form the main pillars in a single, all-purpose North Wirral authority was received coolly by Wallasey, which was believed to favour an all Merseyside and Wirral unitary authority. The paper, which as we have seen was prone to give a good deal of publicity to the Liberal leader, printed a 400 word appeal from him to the public to make their objections to the Maud proposals known. On 18 October the final acceptance of Maud, in general, by the council was reported without comment on an inside page. Another item dealt with the discussions being held by the Council of Social Services on the future of voluntary organisations in the event of reorganisation. The paper's editorial eyes, as ever, were elsewhere – on bonfires and fireworks.

The two Wirral papers responded to the Maud report by giving it a reasonable degree of coverage in the issue after it had appeared, but subsequently they allowed it to die very rapidly as a news area. It cast few ripples over coverage in the succeeding weeks. The papers' attempts to explain on their own initiative why the report was significant was, in the case of Birkenhead, rather feeble; in the case of Wallasey, virtually non-existent. In Wallasey, no newspaper 'attitude' to Maud was manifest at all. The Birkenhead paper, by contrast, was hostile, and made a point of pouring cold water over both Maud and M.A.L.T.S. It may be that both papers reflected the views of their respective political establishments. The Wallasey political establishment was neither for nor against Maud, since its main fear, of domination by Birkenhead, had been reasonably allayed. Birkenhead had had its own hopes of domination (of the Wirral) dashed, and feared for the town's identity in a Liverpool-centred administration, while councillors and officials feared for their positions.

Such fears were equally apparent in the Bootle paper, which in the 1960s had championed the town's autonomy and sought to remould its image. The Report offered Bootle little that was desirable, and was treated accordingly. In Liverpool the most local paper – the *Liverpool Weekly News* – treated the whole affair disdainfully as irrelevant. The *Post* and *Echo* difference of attitude and treatment reflected the problems of papers with a regional and conurban readership – the *Echo*'s editorial welcome being carefully balanced by the prominence given to Chester and Wirral objections.

It may be more important to reflect upon the reception of the Maud Report as a news event. It was, after all, a Royal Commission

Report, not a White Paper or a Bill. While in prospect it represented an event vital to the future of the four boroughs, it was a prospect and *not* an actuality. This may help explain why all the papers allowed the question to arise from nowhere and disappear into limbo in the space of a few issues. As a prospect, Maud exercised the local political élites and the newspapers – except the outsider *Liverpool Weekly News* – reflected their reactions. No paper exerted itself to campaign for or against the proposals, or even to educate its readership into a greater awareness of what was at stake overall.

The public as such hardly reacted. Coverage of the Report was, generally, adequate and we may assume that had there been a mass of letters, many would have been printed and the volume of letters referred to. Readers, possibly, lacked specific information on local implications for them in terms of service provision and better administration – and certainly the coverage did not help very much. Most, like the journalists, must have seen the Report as having only implications for the distant future. Journalists apparently assumed that people could not grasp such sweeping change, did not care and did not believe such change to be practical politics. Whether correct or not in this assumption, the journalists acted upon it and returned to the pressing questions of service provision and party politics. Maud was a seven-day wonder for newspapers and readers.

### THE 'GOOD OF THE TOWN'

The way the newspapers treated routine local government and party political news, and the special kind of news presented by something like the Redcliffe–Maud Report, is sufficiently self-revealing to require little further comment. There was a failure to educate the public in any on-going fashion, but the nature of the news and the way it arose often presented great obstacles to this. As for journalistic and editorial policy, it would be wrong to say that the papers (with one exception) were basically uncommitted. They were committed, but to a rather innocuous concept, the 'good of the town'. Being considered self-evident, it was never really examined in any depth. At best, it involved the attempt to foster community consciousness. At worst it often identified the interest of a section of the townspeople as the interest of all. It was, in both respects, in short, the local equivalent of the hackneyed concept 'the national interest'.

As an editorial guiding principle the 'good of the town' may be expressed as a series of axioms:

1. Business activity is good.
2. Conflict is bad; party conflict especially is contrary to the public interest, unseemly, and largely unnecessary.
3. The Town Hall is doing its best and we must all support it.
4. We – the newspaper – can occasionally criticise the Town Hall and the Council, but only because we understand their problems and basically we are on their side.

# 7

## Editorial perspectives

'Gatekeepers' play a crucial role in any communication process. In the organisation of the local press these are the men who decide what is news and what is to be presented to the public. Much of the responsibility for public information rests with them. We now turn to them, their problems, and their view of the world.

Who were the men principally responsible for what appeared in Merseyside's local press in the 1960s? Who decided how the news and feature pages were filled? Answering these questions meant interviewing the editors of the weeklies, and, in one case, the managing editor as well. On the dailies, the effective day-to-day editor was the news editor and was, in fact, the same man for both papers.

The very experience of meeting editors, with a view to investigating and reporting on the situation from their viewpoint, itself throws light on their problems. They were, to us, what many of their contacts must be to them – people whose courtesy in giving us facts and information had to be respected by a reciprocal courtesy. In some cases, effort had to be made to preserve anonymity. Insightful asides had sometimes to be regarded as not for general publication. With the number of key actors being so few, candid comments would not be hard to track down to their sources. This is, of course, not an uncommon experience in research involving comparatively small groups of public figures. They, in their turn, no doubt exercised a degree of self-censorship in what they chose to reveal to us. What follows is, to some degree, the product of constraints similar to those with which editors live in their relationships with their news-producing public.

The most striking thing about these men was their homogeneity – they were local men, locally educated and locally recruited, trained and promoted. If not actually from Merseyside, then they had followed almost their entire careers there. None had a stint on a national paper behind him and none had any formal higher education. War service apart, their working lives had been spent on Merseyside. One only had gone temporarily out of journalism, and that into public relations.

Monitors of the local world they may claim to be – products of that local world they certainly were. Only one came from outside the ambit of the *Liverpool Daily Post* and *Liverpool Echo* group. He saw himself 'at the top' of his journalistic world. The others, in their various niches, clearly saw their future in the group and, even more so, in the area. National journalists may 'live out of a suitcase'. These local journalists were the very reverse – local men, deeply rooted, working locally. Inertia, one of them remarked, rather rue-fully, 'has to be reckoned with'. From someone over 50 this was, presumably, a statement of fact, not expectation.

The world of the local paper is not likely to be easily influenced by outsiders, even by new ownership from outside. Its key actors are local products reared writing their papers. There are, as we have empha-sised, great differences between the scale of operation of a large provincial daily and a local weekly. The editor of one of our weeklies might rank only with an established reporter on one of the dailies.

Local journalists are men who seem confident that they know their readers, their papers and the roles those papers play in the community. 'The *Birkenhead News*', said its former managing editor (now deceased), 'plays a very important part in the Birken-head community life – a big part in making the town an entity where people know what other people are doing.' And if the paper was important to the town, so was the town to the nation. Birken-head, he said, was 'one of the great county boroughs of England'. Another journalist saw his paper as a 'go-between for disgruntled people and councillors'. The *Post* and *Echo*'s news editor saw his task as a threefold one. Primarily, it was to provide the 'fastest, most accurate, most comprehensive service of news'; secondly, to interpret this through articles; and thirdly to provide comment. While journalists in Liverpool and Birkenhead claimed a 'good cross section' of the community read them, not surprisingly those in Wallasey and Bootle pointed to the lower middle class and working class respectively as the predominant source of their readers. All saw their papers primarily as vehicles for, in this order, social and commercial news and information; political news; and sporting and other news.

'News' to these men was obvious in its nature, if difficult to define. For one editor the touchstone was the 'general good of the people'. Anything that affected it was news. Another stressed that for a weekly 'nothing is too trivial if it is local'. These were two important rules of thumb. Another journalist stressed that for political news there had to be the explicit element of more, or less, taxation in prospect – 'people aren't interested if it doesn't involve their money'. The question 'what is news?' was one that all found distinctly metaphysical. They could not really handle the question, for clearly it had never been thought of in abstract terms. They would know the answer when they saw it, as a matter of practice.

Editors revealed themselves as adherents of a deeply held journalistic ethic. Suggestion that the paper supported one political party or group was denied in an almost reflex fashion. 'We are equally aggressive to them all' said one editor. Probably none of the parties had affection for him, he said, but they might have respect. Another took it as a compliment that each party thought he favoured the other. His town had an acrimonious council but its members were personally friendly to him. He needed good relations with both sides and felt that, in a comparatively small town, having a 'political' line would sour his contacts. In general, editors' attitude to party politics was to regard it as a necessary evil in local government. Several regretted the absence of independent-minded council members. Few were even happy to assent to the notion of supporting the Council 'regardless of party'. What emerged was the affirmation that their papers had the (undefined) good of the town at heart and advanced this chiefly by publishing news and, though much less, by putting their own views.

The news editor of the *Liverpool Daily Post* and *Liverpool Echo* vigorously rebutted the charge of being subservient to an 'establishment' of whatever kind. That charge, he claimed, came from a variety of sources. Some were people who wanted more coverage of certain topics and who would not appreciate that the dailies had a large 'beat', had to spread themselves, and hence had to ignore much 'news' from any *one* area. Others were people who bitterly resented the fact that journalists did have their own ethic, were autonomous, and would not easily be manipulated either into silence or into purveying 'doctored news'. He reeled off a string of large Liverpool companies which, he asserted, had been held, over the years, to be the real editors of the *Daily Post* and *Echo* and declared that, to the contrary, the papers had offended all of them at one time or another. He prided himself on his political coverage, the scoops the dailies achieved, and on their capacity to make the whole system 'leak' news and information.

Plato's 'Guardians' might be an unacknowledged model for journalists. For a small weekly editor this might mean anything from the role of a sympathetic but independent close observer to that of an abrasive 'tribune of the people', a self image held, to some degree, by the editor of the *Liverpool Weekly News*. For a big, bustling daily – well able to take care of itself in the city rough and tumble – the role might carry overtones of news creator and manager in a way not open to smaller papers. This, of itself, might offend some critical circles and might reinforce the presumption that an institution so large and significant could never be objective.

The local journalist, inevitably, operates in a small community and gets much of his information at a price. All the editors gave as their principal news source that of personal contact with senior officials and councillors, especially committee chairmen. They attended committee meetings and press briefings where possible and also relied considerably on circulated material of various kinds. We put it to them that the handling of all information is constrained, in addition to the usual considerations of space, time, and legal considerations, by the necessity to preserve most of their news sources. This was a conception they found difficult to handle. They denied ever restraining themselves to save official face or, even more, the *amour propre* of a councillor or group of councillors. The handling of political news in the local community was not seen as in any sense problematic. Editors were in receipt of as much news as they needed, measured in terms of quantity. Most of them had no disposition to think in terms of its quality. The political apple cart was not going to be upset by investigatory journalism. The relationship with officials was one of trust, so that, one editor put it, if this is infringed 'they [the officers] soon get over their anger'. The same applied with council members, though respect was not unmixed. Some council members were persistent contacters of the dailies. With the weeklies, however, it was comparatively rare for the paper to be directly used by a council member wishing to get something across to the public. On the other hand, most editors subscribed to the view that their presence at council and committee engenders a proportion of its debate and its tenor. Journalistic wisdom was that 'meetings end a few minutes after we leave', and this was often an acid test of the real motives of the performers.

For most of the press, then, the relationship with the Town Hall was a fairly comfortable one. That proximity might lead to some emasculation of the press as an effective news purveyor was a consideration which had clearly not occurred to most of the journalists. In the case of the *Post* and *Echo*, the editor was able to boast a genuine plurality of sources. He could always get the information he wanted. But for the weeklies, the relationship was more simple. They took what they were given, and were grateful for it. The *Birkenhead News* editor summed his position up: 'Anything they're prepared to tell us goes in, but some things they prefer to keep back.' Not so trusting was the editor of the *Liverpool Weekly News*. This paper had the style of an abrasive outsider. It was, in fact, edited by a man who lives and works outside the city and isn't often in Liverpool himself. He claimed to know few city councillors, and clearly preferred this distance from them. For him, local government was full of people seeking 'to cover up (news), not give out'. Greater access to committees and material, he would regard as evidence of better 'public relations' not of anything more. Public relations, he felt, exists to keep news from the public, not to give it. Local authorities never would give access to information likely to bring them into disrepute. The work of the Local Government Information Office clearly fell into this category of activity also. Its latest pamphlet on informing the public was 'eyewash'. He would rather not be taken into the confidence of local government people. This, he feared, might result in the paper 'selling the bosses to the men'; and there was not much doubting that this was precisely what he thought many of his fellow local journalists were doing, wittingly or not. It is not surprising that he thought, with evident satisfaction, that while quite a few councillors had 'quite a respect' for the *Weekly News*, 'as many see us as a bloody nuisance'.

The essential modesty of editors about their relationship to local government, their disinclination (with one exception) to shake things up, emerged in yet another respect. They were not inclined to see their own editorials as of great significance. No 'thunderers' these. On the weeklies, and to an extent on the dailies, the editorial was set up before the front page was finalised. It was quite possible for it to deal with matters unrelated to the main story of the day, however much that might have been a political earthquake. No great effort was made to avoid this. One editor dismissed an editorial as 'the views of one man' rather than the paper, and another very clearly saw it as a useful space to fly the *occasional* kite or prevent an area of policy being submerged by more newsworthy matters. Rightly or wrongly, journalists felt readers generally ignored editorials, though one of them reported being 'heartened' by public response and another editor considered there was increasing interest in this, as in all coverage of local politics in his town. More people were contacting the paper, so perhaps, he thought, it was succeeding.

Working journalists clearly see more significance in front-paging, news-positioning and presentation than in editorials. If the lead story – 'the newsiest item of the week' one called it – is political, then it is because it is 'newsy', that is, he said, 'that item or event which is likely to affect the greatest number in the community'. We saw earlier that politics makes the front page, even the lead story, quite often in some of the papers, and not infrequently in others. For the journalist this is because the 'story' had or could be given a more 'newsy' slant than its competitors for that issue. It was not because the matter was *necessarily* more significant, or that politics was 'owed' a lead for a change.

'Newsiness' can and does mean single appearances of themes which come from the blue and return to it in one issue for a weekly or a couple for a daily. The phenomenon of worthy but 'dead' news was very familiar to the journalists. In the news competition for one issue, X story rates front-paging, if not the lead spot. In the competition for the following issues, X story loses out to Y and Z stories and thus, despite the raised interest of the reader, X may only appear again much later in some retrospective allusion. These local journalists were aware that in political news the hint of political scandal, great redevelopment hopes, fierce committee battles, walk-outs from the council – all may end not with the bang of resolution and information but with the whimper of lame follow up or, often, deafening silence. Journalists all claimed to guard against this – two editors kept files of unfinished news and periodically checked through them. Another remarked ruefully that 'to confess that on X we misunderstood, or that on Y there is nothing now to say is hardly news'. Indeed not. But the problem remains an acute one.

The space given to readers' letters varies greatly between papers, and the weekly journalists claim that this is a reflection of the number of letters received rather than any question of policy. If so, these varied greatly from one public to another. The *Liverpool Weekly News* editor had enough for a whole page or even two per week. On the other hand another of the weeklies claimed to receive very few publishable letters, despite having made great efforts to attract them. Letters are edited to save space and sometimes excluded on legal grounds but, if their bona fides are valid, they can expect to be printed, and not only when there is already a controversy in the area concerned. Some journalists preferred letters from spokesmen of organisations, others expressed caution on 'professional letter writers'. All asserted that, too often, letters were on subjects outside local government and expressed personal ignorance and idiosyncrasy, rather than justified grievance or a useful political contribution. That their papers were seen as general ombudsmen, journalists had little doubt – by letter and telephone the paper's help was solicited fairly widely. Where a 'story' was scented there was a follow up; where not, the query was redirected. Overall, the journalists valued the letter column though their attitude to it was fairly casual. They did not see it as having much political potential.

The 1960s for the journalists was a decade of opportunities and problems. Rising costs of newspaper production meant a drive for brighter papers to attract and retain readers. The availability of the web-offset process on the weeklies meant less dog-work for journalists but tighter time-tables and a more tightly structured existence. On the other hand, it proved too expensive for the Wallasey and Bootle papers and the experiment with it lasted only a year or two. All editors were somewhat ambivalent about the changes in newspaper production. The position of the *Weekly News* illustrates the dilemma of the smaller newspapers faced with the pressures of economics and technical change. It claimed to be one of the first papers in the country to introduce web-offset, and it proposed to continue a process of plant modernisation. At the same time its editor was concerned that the fact that a profit had to be made could easily conflict with good journalism. Many papers were really businesses run by accountants, he felt. He, and others also, regretted a situation in which late copy displeased not merely an editor but, by extension, a computer and, even more, a time-conscious accountant. The latter symbolised a new age; journalists were conscious of being managed as never before and the ambitious among them had to aspire to be skilled technicians in 'communication' not creative writers and, ultimately, managers not editors.

Staff turnover on the weeklies was high. The *Liverpool Daily*

*Post* and *Echo* group had a policy of 'growing its own' on its weeklies, and the *Liverpool Weekly News* lost most juniors once they
were fully fledged journalists – to the *Liverpool Daily Post* and
*Liverpool Echo* team and elsewhere. The weeklies, certainly, and
perhaps even the dailies, were often short of locally knowledgeable,
experienced journalists.

The youth of many of the journalists was striking on all the
papers. The papers appeared to comprise a tiny handful of middle-
aged journalists supervising and directing assistants twenty years
their junior. Most of the latter had come straight from school, from
writing, as one editor put it, for the school magazine to writing for
the local paper. These editors in embryo were experiencing few
influences that were not local. Most college students away from
home have far wider experience than their contemporaries in local
journalism.

None of the weeklies could afford the luxury of a designated
specialist municipal correspondent. With journalistic staffs of only
5 to 10 little specialisation was possible. Generally, the editor plus
one or two of the younger and perhaps a more senior journalist
shared the task of news gathering, sifting and writing up. One
editor, asked how much he thought politics took of reporters' time,
estimated 10 per cent, and less for himself – the others thought
more. He had many other news areas and considerations to bear
in mind. Politics had to take its chance with anything and everything which might be 'news'. One editor confessed to a sense of
obligation to provide political news though 'it's often very dull'.

The editors were optimistic about the future of the local press.
The existence of the large *Liverpool Daily Post* and *Liverpool Echo*
group of papers meant that the papers could mirror their boroughs,
while the journalists had no real fear themselves that local government boundary changes might put their paper in jeopardy. In spite
of technical change, these men felt 'there will always be room for a
local paper'.

Similarly local radio caused no great concern. There was the
conviction that, while it might marginally affect news presentation, the audience was still small and radio was no substitute for
lengthy, written analysis which could be savoured and pondered
over. The possibility of local commercial radio is obviously a
different matter, potentially threatening, as it was felt to do, the
economic viability of the papers. The *Weekly News* editor said no

demand for it had existed. It was being forced on the country quite cynically by people anxious to make money. The *Liverpool Daily Post* and *Liverpool Echo* group readied themselves for the challenge of participating in the new development.

Editors were asked to discuss their view of the political problems of each of their towns. Table 12 indicates their response to questioning about local authority services, and this should be seen in conjunction with the results of content analysis given in chapter 5. Column C is a reminder of the three services found to have been given most coverage during the 1960s in each of the papers. Column A gives editors' rankings of services in order of their importance as sources of newsworthiness.

Table 12. *Editors and service coverage*

|  | Bootle T.H. | | | Birkenhead News | | | Wallasey News | | | Liverpool D.P. & E. | | | Liverpool W.N. | | |
|---|---|---|---|---|---|---|---|---|---|---|---|---|---|---|---|
|  | A | B | C | A | B | C | A | B | C | A | B | C | A | B | C |
| Education | 2 | L | 1 | 1 | H | 1 | 3 | H | 2 | 3 | H |  | 2 | H | 2 |
| Housing | 1 | H | 2 | 2 | H |  | 2 | A |  | 3 | H | 2 | 1 | H | 1 |
| Transport |  | A |  | 3 | A |  | 2 | H | 1 | 4 | A |  |  | H |  |
| Highways |  | L |  |  | L | 3 |  | A |  | 5 | L | 3 |  | A |  |
| Planning | 5 | A | 3 | 3 | A | 2 |  | H | 3 | 4 | L | 1 |  | H | 3 |
| Police | 4 | L |  | 4 | L |  |  | A |  | 1 | L |  | 3 | L |  |
| Fire |  | L |  |  | L |  |  | A |  | 2 | L |  | 4 | L |  |
| Welfare |  | A |  | 4 | A |  | 5 | A |  | 4 | L |  |  | A |  |
| Children |  | L |  |  | L |  |  | L |  | 5 | L |  | 5 | H |  |
| Finance |  | H |  |  | H |  | 1 | H |  | 5 | A |  |  | H |  |
| Health | 3 | L |  |  | H |  | 4 | A |  |  | L |  |  | H |  |
| Libraries |  | L |  |  | L |  | 1 | L |  | 5 | L |  |  | L |  |
| Water |  | L |  | 5 | L |  |  | L |  |  | L |  |  | A |  |
| Cleansing |  | L |  |  | L |  |  | L |  |  | L |  |  | L |  |

A = Editors' ranking of newsworthiness.
B = Editors' ranking of controversiality (H = High, A = Average, L = Low).
C = Rank order of service in actual coverage 1962–69 (see Table 9, p. 67).

Column B indicates whether the service was rated high, average or low as a matter of controversy in the town. In some cases, such as finance and planning, much depended on definition. In Wallasey, finance was clearly taken to mean an all-embracing

rather than a highly specific activity. Newsworthiness and controversiality do not necessarily go together. Education in Bootle,
though as elsewhere considered highly newsworthy, was considered
of low controversiality. It was, said the editor 'a kid-conscious town'.
His paper certainly reflected this view, but accompanied it with
the editorial line that educational controversy was something the
town could not afford. It might be added that, as a town without
any long-standing grammar schools to be defended, educational
controversy was comparatively easy to avoid.

More generally, how did his town and its politics seem from the
editor's chair? Birkenhead, during this period, was notable for the
consistency with which the Labour leader was presented as the
key to politics. In particular he was considered to have done a skilled
political job in achieving a favourable outcome for the town in the
negotiations over the siting of the second Mersey tunnel. The
town's chief problem, apart from the housing problem, was considered to be the way traffic congestion had 'brought the town
almost to a standstill'. The paper had tried to bring attention to
these problems. The editor thought people were getting more
interested in the town's affairs, owing, he thought, to the upheavals
of recent years. The *Wallasey News*'s editor stressed the 'growing
inadequacy' of public transport in the town, and considered that
the paper's campaigns in the 1960s had drawn attention to the dis-
tress caused by this and had achieved some results. He was less
satisfied with the paper's performance in the field of housing. The
paper, he claimed, had consistently complained that the new
estates in the town's west end were 'simply addresses' with in-
sufficient amenities, civic pride, etc.; but they had not got very far
with this. The Bootle editor considered his a town which had
missed few of its available opportunities in the 1960s and yet which
had succeeded in maintaining its traditions. Bootle, he said, was
'building today the town of tomorrow'. Although he agreed to the
suggestion that British towns were often run by small groups of
people, he denied that this was so of Bootle. Nevertheless he
acknowledged the campaigning role of the present Town Clerk
and his predecessor in bringing changes about. The editors of the
Liverpool papers were, not unnaturally, more prone to see the city
in a national context. The *Post* and *Echo* news editor was aware
of being, to a degree, the 'voice of Merseyside' in London. He had
campaigned on a range of the usual local issues – roads, road

safety, a learn-to-swim campaign. He had championed the cause of a maritime museum. But he was also concerned with how the area looked from the outside. Its image, and particularly its unfavourable reputation for industrial unrest and vandalism, were matters of great concern to him. He felt the city was not conscious enough of the importance of its image. In this context it may be noted that although he denied that the city was run by a small group of people he was prepared to single out the planning officers, Mr Graeme Shankland and his successors, as being officials playing a notable role in creating change in the city. The modernisation of the city and the labour problems in its industries were also the issues mentioned by the *Weekly News* editor. He would have liked, had he had the staff, to have given more of a lead to his readers, many of whom worked in key industries with labour problems. There was a grave danger that a badly advised and led labour force could lead to Liverpool 'going down the drain'. He acknowledged the need to redevelop and modernise the city, but he was worried that the process could go too far and destroy what was of value, particularly community life.

In general, editors' choice of local problems stressed the image of their town, and they saw physical renewal as the key to the future. But they were aware of the costs of change, particularly the loss of 'community' in areas about to change or areas recently built, and it was in this respect that they seemed most alive to a sense of the social.

This brief examination of the situation as viewed from six editorial chairs affords some clues as to the forces which make up the local newspaper's style of approaching local politics. The potential range of surveillance of the political scene is limited by a number of important constraints operating on Merseyside journalists and, almost certainly, on local journalists elsewhere.

First, there is the constraint of resources. With the exception of the *Post* and *Echo*, these were very small-scale operations. The newspapers had only very limited capacity to do other than accept the standard routine of writing up 'what was said' in council and committee, plus what could be culled from hand-outs and annual reports. In turn this meant that no one on the staff was able to build up the kind of knowledge that might give him a base for authoritative criticism of what was going on. On political issues the paper could voice the views of the man in the street because it was written by people who, in terms of political knowledge, *were* the men in the street. Its capacity to inform, however, was really little more than a capacity to transmit information raw.

Secondly, the independence of editors vis-à-vis local politics was constrained because they were, as we have seen, men who had had almost no experience of any world other than that of their own town. In terms of Robert Merton's local–cosmopolitan dimension these were locals. Locals in origin, locals in thought. This is not necessarily a bad thing. There is much to be said for a paper having an instinctive 'sense of the town'. The one attempt which was made during the 1960s to import an outsider (from Fleet Street) into a leading position in one of the papers, the *Birkenhead News*, did not have altogether happy results, either inside the paper as an organisation or among the readership, who preferred the more conventional if less lively style of the paper as it had been. But an exclusively local editorial staff may suffer, unwittingly, from several disadvantages. The most obvious danger is of being incorporated into the Town Hall ambit and becoming its vehicle, or of being in an over-close sympathy with particular local individuals or interests. Closeness to sources is a problem in any case. Many potential stories must be lost because in a small scale situation the source might be easily traceable. This may account for some of the blandness of coverage. But the chief danger is more that 'locals', lacking alternative experience, may be un-selfaware. They may accept as normal and inevitable what, to an outsider, may seem highly questionable. The possibility that there might be something problematic in the pattern of their relationships, in the way they decided on 'news', gathered it and reported it, did not appear to make sense to several (though not all) of the editors. That they might be obliged to do things in a certain way is one thing. It is quite another that they were unable to grasp that the possibility of alternatives was, at least, a real question.

This leads to the third constraint, the existence of, and journalists' socialisation into, a set of 'rules of the game', which lays down what local politics is supposed to be about and what press reporting of it is about. Each generation of new reporters is inducted into the routine of news gathering, the whole business of editing verbatim reports of council meetings, extracting snippets from reports, getting quick telephoned quotes from leading people. This routine is internalised; it becomes inconceivable to break away from it. There is little time to go beyond this basic raw material, and to do so might be resented among councillors and officials jealous of their autonomy. Fleet Street might be a 'fourth estate', but the local press is too weak and too close to the other estates in the local scene to be capable of joining them. The young journalist drinks this understanding in with his first cups of coffee. He is not knowledge-able, and there is a certain premium on him not becoming know-ledgeable.

Journalists also learn to act on two premises which stem both from popular perceptions of local government and from the nature of the material they are handling. The first of these is that local government is dull, and that reporting it is a matter of civic duty rather than natural inclination. Most of the editors appeared to lean towards this point of view. It is clearly impossible to say how much coverage is given *purely* out of a sense of duty, but if this is a notion which informs the whole attitude to local government it must be very hard for a beginner in journalism not to make it his own, especially since, vicious circles being what they are, he almost certainly is already predisposed to this view.

Secondly, editors confirmed the view with which we concluded our reading of their papers, namely that they believe in something real called 'the good of the town'. The papers stood for this 'good of the town' and were in favour of anything that could be associated with this concept. Talking to them, we saw how signifi-cant in their minds was the question of the image of the towns, how in fact it was essentially a concern over image which gave the 'good of the town' its force. Redevelopment was good for the town, less for its substantive benefits than because it was in keeping with the notion of 'a progressive town'. Bad housing was emphasised less on account of the human misery it represented than because it was not in keeping with a good image. Educational progress was 'good for the town'; the switch to comprehensives generally aroused apprehension less on educational grounds than because it was a cause of party conflict which was 'bad for the town'. Parties were asknowledged by the editors as a necessary evil, justifiable at best on the grounds of helping to create interest. Considerable cynicism was expressed by some about councillors' motives. One said they 'do not want to know us except at election time'.

Detachment from the parties and attachment to the 'good of the town' as *the* political good leads in most cases to the adoption of, at best, 'consensus politics', in which the paper supports the highest common political factor between the parties; and at worst to non-politics, the avoidance of any kind of political stance whatever.

Editorial non-politics is, of course, a kind of politics. Let us now examine how the press was viewed in turn by people active in local party politics and town government.

# 8

# The press and local politicians

Local party politics is the continuous concern of a comparatively
small number of people. How do they view the local press? Do
they consider it gives adequate coverage of local government and
politics? Do they consider it biased as between parties, despite its
own claims to neutrality? Are there major differences in the view
they take of the local press from one town to another?

It would, of course, have been desirable to ask these, and other,
questions, of a sample of the general readership, as well as of the
political activists. It may be inferred from other surveys, notably
the Maud Report, that for the present writers, such an exercise
would not have been cost-effective, bringing comparatively weak
returns for a considerable outlay in effort. Of that minority of
people who are really active in the local political system, 175 were,
however, questioned. They are clearly unrepresentative of the
general public as a whole. But they are representative of a critically
important public in so far as the local press relates to politics. As a
sample of the activists in politics, they are among the most know-
ledgeable about the system the press is trying to report. As subjects
of reportage themselves, the press's approach is of great concern to
them. At the outset one might hypothesise that their actions, from
time to time, might be taken specifically in the light of their
knowledge of press publicity and of its character. For them at least,
political coverage, its quality and quantity, its partisanship, the
stances adopted, *is* important, and different in import from petty
crime or the weekly sporting routine.

The 175 surveyed were 26 aldermen and 86 councillors, with
63 'activists', usually chairmen or secretaries of ward parties,
spread throughout the four boroughs. Eighty-three were Conservatives and associates, 80 Labour, and 11 Liberals, with one Com-
munist. Because of the balance of party control locally at the time
of survey, 1969–70, the Conservatives included a higher proportion of councillors and aldermen than Labour. The difference in
attitude between the two categories, on and off the councils, was
negligible.

124

All the council members and activists proved to be readers of the local paper of their town. In addition, between a third and a half read one or other of the Liverpool dailies, and especially the *Liverpool Echo* – read by 93 of the 112 council members. The *Liverpool Weekly News* appears to have a peculiar status, being read by only half the Liverpool respondents, and even some of these having, occasionally, to be reminded of its existence before affirming their readership. It is read by about as many as read the other weeklies, but this means that in relation to the city of Liverpool it must rank as comparatively small beer.

A considerable degree of dissatisfaction with the press's coverage of local government was expressed. Asked about the main papers, the *Liverpool Daily Post* and the *Liverpool Echo*, only five respondents considered their coverage 'very good'; 60 considered it 'good'; and 101 thought it 'not very good'. Liberals appeared to be notably more satisfied than members of the two large parties, in each of which the majority were dissatisfied. The weeklies in the outer boroughs were even less favourably viewed, only some 20 per cent of councillors in the outer boroughs approving the coverage of their local weekly paper.

When respondents were asked to explain some of the reasons why they felt as they did, there proved to be no lack of these. Among those who viewed the coverage favourably or very favourably, the explanations, broadly speaking, fell into two categories, namely, the situation of the press as they saw it, and the attitudes of the readers. In respect of the former, a large number of the well-disposed agreed with the Birkenhead Conservative Councillor that 'given the restrictions on space they do pretty well'. Regarding the latter, many were very clear that, in the words of another Birkenhead Conservative, the papers did well considering '80 per cent of the people find local politics boring'.

Among the dissatisfied both these considerations were grounds of complaint, and other grounds were added. In fact, a series of attitudes emerged which are worth examining.

Firstly, perhaps inevitably, there was the charge of distortion for a variety of reasons. Most of our respondents, and especially councillors and aldermen, had long had dealings with the press. Accordingly, they had learnt that there could be a wide gap between what they thought they had said and how, and in what context, their words actually appeared. A large number in all parties claimed to see much distortion. A Bootle Conservative Councillor put this down to the fact that 'the papers condense it [a story] so much that it is out of context'. A Birkenhead Liberal asserted that distortion was normal when reports of council, for example, consisted of 'chunks of minutes' rather than coherent accounts.

Not all were prepared to see such distortion as a product of the demands on newspaper space or limitation of resources. Some looked for reasons in the area of 'news creation' by journalists, and in a very direct sense. Some of our respondents spoke of being interviewed by reporters who seemed to have already written their piece, and who were seeking names to make it seem authentic. As one Liverpool Labour activist noted wryly, 'When he [the reporter] says "What you're saying is . . ." then look out, for what he's about to say is not, or not quite, what you have said.' The same man, and others, cited similar occasions, though with the difference that in those there was active collusion between journalists and publicity seekers. Another Labour activist noted 'They push for controversy and for easy news. They stage events, and connive with news seekers to get the news.'

In the second place there was the assertion of a failure by the newspapers to give a lead in local politics, to 'give meaning to events' or to rise above, in the words of one Birkenhead Liberal, merely 'giving establishment views and disregarding or distorting other views'. A Liverpool Labour activist asserted that the press position in the 'civic establishment prevents them from being anything but unheroic and content with non-controversial treatment of issues'. A Birkenhead Liberal saw it as a duty of the press to 'inject some life into local questions'. He wanted a 'more positive editorial approach' and an end to what he saw as the clearly visible stance of 'never be rude to those in power'. A Conservative from the same town accused the press of being full of 'trite rubbish' and resignedly noted that 'Local rags, as a name, suits them beautifully.'

The third attitude held that not only was no lead given, but that the stuff of local politics was not adequately communicated to the people. In the words of a Liverpool Labour councillor the press fails to 'endow local politics with news value'. This respondent agreed with the Bootle Conservative councillor who commented that the press 'blows up trivia and ignores sound, solid stuff. It seldom reports what the public wants to know.' The general criticism was elaborated by more specific accusations of a lack of 'background on policy areas or on party developments' (Liverpool Labour).

Along with this went the charge – more technical but vital – that the newspapers lacked quality reporters or, at least, well-trained reporters who could interest first their editors, and then the public. One Liverpool Labour councillor cited a former reporter on one of the weeklies as a rarity in that 'he managed to present local events in a way that interested his editor'. He had had 'an eye for significance'. By contrast, most journalists lacked such an eye so far as local politics was concerned; for them 'unless I hit the Chairman [of a committee] it is not news'.

The widespread acceptance of one or more of these attitudes by those who were dissatisfied (the great majority) clearly indicated their disregard for the local press as a serious source of reliable fact or opinion, though there was ample testimony to its capacity for mischievous use of both. Even those favourably disposed believed this to an extent. One of these, a Birkenhead Conservative, referred to the press as 'sometimes useful, though it tells me nothing I don't know'. Two Liverpool Labour activists spoke for those less well disposed. One, who confessed himself a voracious reader, noted 'I use it as an insurance policy in case I miss something.' Another, a Liverpool councillor, unequivocally assessed the value of the press as a local news source as being 'only for gossip, but that is valuable to a politician'.

All of the papers see themselves as politically independent. Indeed, we have noted that the ideology of political independence appears to be important to editors. Nor have we reason to doubt that this is genuinely and sincerely held. The council members and party activists, those with most to gain or lose by partisan support from the local paper, did not appear to hold the same picture of the paper as the newspapermen themselves. Only a minority see no party bias. Did the *Liverpool Daily Post* and the *Liverpool Echo* seem to lean towards one party, we asked? Thirty-six respondents saw no such leaning, three saw a leaning to Labour, 48 to the Liberals and 67 to the Conservatives. Most, though not all, of those who saw no party bias were Conservatives. Labour and Liberal respondents were disposed to see the papers supporting the Conservative party. The Liberal leaning was largely a Conservative perception, especially so in Liverpool itself.

When respondents were asked to illustrate the nature of the

partisanship they claimed to see or not see, the answers were revealing. Conservatives spoke of the press favour being extended, as one put it, to 'articulate, publicity-seeking Liberals'. Labour activists who saw pro-Conservative bias, if not an anti-Labour stance as such, referred frequently to 'distortion and misrepresentation'. One Liverpool Labour activist typified many such comments when he said that 'you can predict the meetings that are not reported or are misrepresented'. Running parallel with such comments went others indicating frustration with the *kind* of press available. A Liverpool Labour councillor, who saw both Liverpool dailies as 'desperately pro-Liberal', went on to add that 'what we lack is an alternative to the Liberal cheap press'. Another Liverpool Labour activist saw no 'discernible party bias' in the several local papers he took. His charge – and variants of it were quite common – was of 'bias by omission'. They failed, he said, to 'investigate the areas of need in schools, the social services, labour relations'. They were, he said, 'supine papers' and, as such, biased to the status quo and the Conservative Party.

While we must accept that these perceptions are of some significance in colouring the political game in the four towns, the meaning of the findings is open to speculation. It is well-nigh impossible to raise the possibility of 'bias' without predisposing the respondent to agree that it exists. At the time of survey, a newspaper disposition to support the government of the town, regardless of party, would have tended to the advantage of the Conservatives, incumbent controlling party in three out of four towns. The Liberal Party, locally no less than nationally, has tended to gain far more publicity than its representative strength, strictly speaking, would warrant, and many of the respondents of the two main parties have tended to see this as a newspaper policy choice favouring the Liberals rather than a natural consequence of the definition of news, leading journalists to highlight the less routine features of the political scene. It is possible, too, that Liberals may, indeed, be more skilled at exploiting means of publicity, partly because of their lack of other channels for the absorption of their energies or partly because of the character of their leading figures. Several Labour respondents noted this. Observation of newspaper coverage suggests that this pro-Liberal tendency, if present, was not particularly marked. It might also be suggested that for some newspaper offices to look kindly upon the Liberals *is* a mark of political neutrality since, in some senses, the Liberals may not be considered as 'counting'. What almost all activists are agreed on is that the papers are not pro-Labour. Some Labour activists go further and allege the press is anti-Labour.

It is clear from the responses that to assent to the notion that the paper 'leans' towards one or other party is not necessarily connected with a complaint of inadequate coverage of local council and political affairs. Among activists for example, 21 people said their local paper was 'good' or 'very good' in its coverage, but 17 of these 21 nevertheless agreed that the paper was slanted in favour of a party.

As between parties and towns, Labour respondents were most disposed to be critical of the quality of coverage; Liberals, though few were in the sample, least. There seemed a somewhat greater readiness to impute bias to the Liverpool papers than to those of the three outer boroughs, though in no case did a majority of respondents reply that there was no political bias. Dissatisfaction with the coverage of local politics was widespread, but perhaps greatest in Birkenhead, where all the Councillors and Aldermen replying to the question (21) said the *Birkenhead News* was 'not very good' in its coverage.

Respondents in Bootle were more critical of the coverage of the Liverpool dailies than those in the other towns, and there does indeed seem to be a tendency for Bootle to get less coverage than the other towns from the dailies.

How did politicians view the question (see chapter 2), of greater press access to their meetings? Leading aldermen were far from happy at the idea of opening up committees to the press. It was felt that on the full council, as things already stood, speeches were very carefully rehearsed and aimed at press publicity. A leading committee chairman in Liverpool (Conservative) felt that the presence of press and public inhibits members, or worse, encourages them, though he would not be averse to their presence at 'uncontroversial' meetings. A colleague of his pointed out that councillors have to take oaths, a responsibility no one else has. But the view was far from unanimous. Another leading committee chairman in Liverpool, again Conservative, would admit the public where collective activities are under debate, such as transportation, but would exclude them when matters relating to persons came up. On the latter point, indeed, agreement was widespread.

Radio Merseyside, opened in 1967, was one of the earliest B.B.C. local radio stations. We took the opportunity of sounding our sample of councillors and aldermen. They were, broadly speaking, overwhelmingly in favour of the station but, almost as strongly, doubtful as to its impact on local politics. About 80 per cent testified to its worthwhileness and about the same proportion would support the continuance of the local authority subsidy. As a vehicle of political communication, its potential is evident. Of those replying to the question, 39 out of 104 council members had themselves broadcast on the station, some quite frequently. Indeed, a majority of the Liverpool councillors in the sample, 22 out of 38, had broadcast. But only a tiny minority would acknowledge being regular listeners, while over 40 per cent had never heard the station at all. Many of these would, no doubt, have been unable to do so, as the service was restricted to V.H.F. channels; there were also many who frankly admitted the pre-eminent claims of other radio and T.V. channels on what spare time they had. Only a third (29) of the respondents considered that the station had any impact on local politics. Radio Merseyside, then, was considered by local politicians as worthy of support, but of little account as a contributor to local political debate.

We have here, then, an indication of how Merseyside's local press is viewed, as to its coverage of local government and politics, by the most interested of its publics for this type of news. A majority of them respond positively to the suggestion that the papers are not politically neutral, and this is especially so amongst Labour Party respondents, who see their party as comparatively friendless where the press is concerned. How we interpret these findings depends as much on our view of the psyches of politicians of different parties as on our assessment as neutral observers of the press's political roles. What emerges with much greater clarity is the view, held by over three-quarters of this sample of those most involved in running Merseyside's politics and local government, that press coverage is inadequate. No doubt the sources of dissatisfaction vary from party to party and town to town. And no doubt the proviso should be made that all activists in any sphere of involvement are likely to feel they should get bigger and better coverage. But politicians operate in the light of their perceptions of their environment, of which the press is part, whether these perceptions are valid or not.

# 9

# Conclusion

Local institutions are to liberty what primary schools are to science; they put it within people's reach; they teach people to appreciate its peaceful enjoyment and accustom them to make use of it.

de Tocqueville[1]

Civic affairs . . . are hardly ever among the main preoccupations of the people who run the newspaper. Out of a sense of duty and for public relations reasons these people want to display a community service attitude. To display the attitude is usually enough, however; the paper need not actually serve the community. Indeed, to do so would as a rule require incurring costs that even a large and prosperous newspaper would not be willing to afford in the name of public service . . .

Banfield and Wilson[2]

A range of justifications may be put forward for having local systems of government: not the least of these is the argument that the claims of democracy demand it. Yet in Britain, and indeed elsewhere, the health of local political systems has long been considered defective by virtue of the apathy and ignorance which persists in a large measure in the citizen body. It is a question that has engaged commentators from John Stuart Mill to the Maud Committee. Now, there are more substantial changes afoot in the way the country is run at the local level than at any time in the last eighty years. A new system of local government is being established. Within it there will have to be taken decisions which will affect, in a wide range of ways, the lives we live and the character of our society. In recent years we might cite as examples the questions of school reorganisation and the redevelopment of old neighbourhoods. While these still remain unresolved, there are oncoming decisions to be made on important issues such as urban traffic and public transportation, and many others.

Increasingly there are signs that many people are disturbed at the prospect of these decisions being taken by officials and politicians operating in isolation from the public. Hence the growth of attempts to create a new politics of community action and hence, too, the general acknowledgement, embodied in Skeffington, of the need to structure planning processes in such a way as to allow for public participation.

If democracy at the local level is to be revitalised, the public must be in receipt of a ready flow of information about what is going on in their community. If this information is to become a useful tool for participation, it must be comprehensive in its nature, dealing with both current happenings and with the backgrounds to them; it must be presented in a readable form and yet not mislead or trivialise; and as much as possible it ought to be based on assessment which is independent of the main sources, so that it is not perverted into a mechanism for managing public opinion. Not all of this need come through the medium of the local press. All possible channels ought to be utilised. But, inevitably, in the foreseeable future the bulk of the responsibility must rest with the local newspaper.

We have attempted to explore how the six Merseyside papers measured up to this responsibility during the 1960s. Analysis of the content of the papers showed that while there could be comparatively little ground for complaint about the proportion of the papers devoted to news of local government and politics, much of the coverage given was hardly of a kind likely to 'encourage enthusiasm, and inculcate in more people the desire to play a part in making each community a better place in which to live'.[3] It was largely made up of small snippets from reports and minutes or heavily personalised accounts of council or committee conflict. Much of it was highly routine matter, some was essentially trivial. The problem was less that important issues were shirked, than that it seemed almost impossible to impart a large amount of information without being either too detailed or too dull for all but the most avid of readers. Like Beith in Oxford and Banbury, we in Merseyside found a heavy dependence on 'received material whether the official "line" of the council . . . the expressed view of councillors, or the public statements of parties and pressure groups'.[4] Some services of local government got almost no publicity at all. Examination of how the papers treated some specific 'stories' or issues revealed, in general, a rather cautious attitude to local political affairs. Often where leadership might have been expected the public were given bromides. Rarely did the papers disturb the

# Conclusion

political atmosphere with revelations based on their own investigations. Almost never was there a report of a case of maladministration or neglect on the part of the council, or of an intra-party dispute, unless it would have emerged into the light of day in any case, through the usual means of official reports or speeches in open council. In the terms of Charles Wright's schema we would have to conclude that the Merseyside local press played a generally functional role vis-à-vis the local political élites.[5] The latter had little to fear from the press, through the exposure of uncomfortable realities. Their legitimacy, and on the whole what they chose to do with it, was endorsed. However, for the individual citizen, much of newspaper output could be regarded as dysfunctional. He got a lot of information, but much of it in a form which cannot have helped understanding. His critical faculties were hardly strengthened by the generally bland or timid manner of editorial surveillance. It is perhaps an untestable hypothesis that this was 'narcotising', but it would be difficult to sustain the contrary argument that the press was a major stimulator of citizen political participation.

journalists with an apolitical attitude, summed up, as he quotes, in
    Of particular significance was the papers' (with one exception) attitude to conflict and controversy. They appeared to believe in a world in which the answers to problems, if not self-evident, were susceptible of yielding to the scrutiny of 'reasonable' men. They either seemed unaware of the existence of inherent conflicts of interests between different groups in the towns, or they chose to report politics as if these did not exist. Conflicts were dutifully reported; but the stress was almost always on the effects, rarely the causes. It was rare for the papers to take sides openly. Usually an appeal to reason, to 'the good of the town', a plea against immoderate language, was made. This provided, in many cases, a convenient way of appearing to make a constructive contribution without having to offend anyone by actually offering a lead to public opinion. Beith, in his study, noted a similar pattern, and exempted journalists from the 'charge' of any overt political bias. Given our conclusions, it is noteworthy that, in effect, he charges journalists with an apolitical attitude, summed up, as he quotes, in the statement, 'Running the town demands honest common sense. not party bickering.'[6] Whether journalism creates or merely reflects this posture the result is clear – the local press is on the side of quiet, orderly government.

133

One of the six newspapers had a conspicuously different attitude to the reporting of political controversy. Where the others regarded the problems of Town Hall with sympathy and tried to interpret it to the people, the *Weekly News* held no brief for Town Hall. It was more of a 'people's paper', for *us* against *them*. Where the other weeklies had a trickle of letters per week, the *Weekly News* had a flood – and rarely printed less than a full page of them. While it ignored much that was going on, it went far beyond the others in its coverage of certain issues, notably housing and the redevelopment of working-class areas. It was not interested in 'balance'. In its stance of noisy advocacy of 'the people' against the 'bureaucrats' it had at times a touchingly old-fashioned air about it. This paper was not bland. It injected into its coverage of politics an element of passion. Readers were left in no doubt of the importance of the decisions taken in local politics, or of the importance of attempting to influence them.

We would not advocate that all local papers adopted the stance of the *Liverpool Weekly News*, since many important areas received no coverage at all. Having as constituency not a whole town or city but only a particular section of it both socially and geographically, it was freer than others to concentrate on covering a smaller range of issues affecting that section – the south Liverpool working class – who were its main readers. But this case does demonstrate that it is possible for a small organisation to produce a paper reporting on local government and politics with verve.

All of the papers did, however, pursue campaigns on matters of public concern, particularly those which were non-party political. All of them made periodic efforts at imparting background information on local government and its services. We should also acknowledge that the papers were improved productions, by 1970, compared with even five or six years earlier, and that this improvement has continued since the end of the study period. The improvement has been most marked in the three borough weeklies, which now have better layout, clearer print, and are livelier to read than in the early sixties, though in some cases at the expense of quantity of material. More attempts are now being made to write features on local matters, using reporters' own leg-and-pen work. Editorial comment is somewhat less arcane. There has been less scope for change in the dailies, though the evening *Echo* has acquired an editorial column, makes more use of its municipal correspondent, and contains more informational articles. But there has been little basic change in the structure of newspaper–local government–reader relationships. This may, however, come about in the near future.

REPORTING LOCAL AFFAIRS: CONSTRAINING FACTORS

Many factors operate together to produce the particular character of press reporting of local affairs which we have examined in this study. Firstly, we must not automatically assume that people, in the smaller centres at least, want editors to 'print the news and raise hell', as Wilbur Storey of the *Chicago Times* put it. Because the papers *are* local, they are very much bound up with local social relationships, which exert powerful inhibiting pressures against any papers disposed to stir up controversy. There is some reluctance to risk the enmity of local political leaders. At worst this could lead to action for libel, which could damage a paper's local standing and finances. Local papers, unlike their national counterparts, do not keep legal advice on tap. Better, normally, to play safe. A more common anxiety, though journalists strenuously deny it, must be the need to retain cooperative sources. The Liverpool dailies are produced by an organisation and in a city large enough for both sides to have a range of different contacts on any point they are interested in; but the other papers in the smaller boroughs operate on a small scale and in a small world in which dependence on access to key sources can be acute. Dislike of what was printed by a member of the political hierarchy could lead to the drying up of certain sources. No doubt cases of this type account for some of the instances of cool local authority/press relations which occur from place to place. In our conversations with local journalists they were disposed to discount fear for sources as a factor in their lives; but it may be suggested that this was so because their resources, and the internalised norms of their profession, meant that it never arose as an active issue, but lay beneath the surface, in the structure of their situation.

There is a second inhibition arising from the perceived nature of the community. Local councillors are not remote figures existing in a world of T.V. and radio and the national papers. Many are well-known local personalities, with many friends among the newspaper's readers, and, possibly, including the editor himself. Local councillors are, for the most part, people who devote a great deal of time and energy to the service of the community – on average 70 hours a month. The work is both voluntary and unpaid. Newspapermen in the smaller towns might well feel reluctant to run the risk of seeming to carp at individuals who have given long service to the town; this may even include a reluctance to ask probing questions about what they are doing. Nor should it be assumed that their public would want them to do so. The public of one small American town, according to a survey, preferred its papers to print 'the facts' rather than take up positions on highly controversial issues. They did not want the newspaper to polarise community attitudes. They wanted it to criticise the council as a whole, but not the individual members. They wanted it to play the watchdog, checking council projects to see that public money was properly spent; publicising lawbreaking; and disclosing 'the facts' about graft and corruption – though without necessarily assuming the responsibility for discovering them. The authors of this survey conclude that in the sense that the public stressed consensus rather than conflict values, they appeared to identify more with the notion of a 'community' rather than a 'journalist' editor.[7] Small town America is, of course, a many faceted reality, and these findings do not hold true for other communities there, let alone in Britain. But they are suggestive of one possible newspaper/community relationship. It may be that an editor who knows his public, will impose limitations upon his own role which may have the effect of blunting any critique of the local political scene he might otherwise have been disposed to offer.

Thirdly, there appears to be a view widely held in local political élite circles that the town must present a favourable image to outsiders. This may especially be the case of towns in regions suffering from their past industrial histories. Essential to this favourable image appears to be the notion of everyone 'pulling together', not 'rocking the boat' etc. Bootle is a good example but all the smaller boroughs showed traces of this. While politics is seen as a necessity, too sharp political controversy over issues of community concern is seen as regrettable. It is felt that the town must not appear divided and it is therefore pictured as one where public spirited men are courageously tackling problems and building a bright future. The majority of our editors were men who either genuinely believed that this was so, or who believed it necessary to promote such an impression.

A fourth factor is the local press's heavy reliance on raw, unprocessed pieces of 'news'. 'A newspaper without opinion', writes

John Whale, 'would be a strange, flabby mutation.'[8] As we have seen, the local press on Merseyside is not exactly without opinion, but a high proportion of it is extremely bland and inoffensive, and we have noted occasions when it was absent altogether when leadership of public opinion might have been expected. In the case of the local paper this relative absence of opinion and interpretative writing is the more a loss because of the 'news' material. This may be a rather extreme form of a characteristic of British journalism in general. On the British national press, Henri Pierre, London correspondent of *Le Monde*, writes

There is, I feel, too much raw news in the British press, and there are too few interpretative news stories. I assume this to be due to the tradition, long held and rigorously observed, of separating news from comment, in order to maintain maximum objectivity. But the mere selection of news, of its size and place in the newspaper infringes that principle. Too many quality newspapers content themselves with giving the maximum of facts, but no more than that, and news without interpretation, divorced from its context, does not mean much.[9]

Another criticism of the British national press is that it is excessively disposed to high frequency news coverage, that is, to the coverage of events or scheduled happenings. Things that have to be 'dug out' because they lie below the surface or because they are part of the structure of things, receive comparatively little attention. If this is a valid criticism of Fleet Street, it is the more so of the local press. In both cases, the economic structure of the industry has much to do with it.

Fifthly, size of the newspaper organisation, in relation to the range of surveillance it is expected to offer, is one of the main reasons why local politics is not reported in a fuller and more penetrating fashion in the weekly papers. The Merseyside weekly papers have journalistic staffs of only 5 to 10 people each. The division of labour between them is, inevitably, fairly undeveloped. Apart from the editor and, perhaps, his assistant, the reporters are generally very junior men of comparatively slight experience. The senior men are too preoccupied with general editorial work, and the juniors too inexperienced and too unspecialised, to be able between them to provide a service of coverage that would bear comparison with the national press's lobby correspondents and political columnists. It is hardly surprising that they are forced to rely upon verbatim accounts of council meetings and snippets from committee papers and annual reports. An equivalent situation on the national press would exist if Fleet Street were dependent on undigested chunks of Hansard and White Papers.

Moreover, and sixthly, the structure of the newspaper industry militates against local papers providing specialist reporting. Nothing is more certain than that if a junior shows promise he will be in line for a transfer to a higher division within the profession – from the weekly to the provincial daily and on to Fleet Street, or to one of the other branches of the profession such as magazine publishing, broadcasting or public relations. Alternatively he may go up within the local weekly world – but again in this case he would be unavailable for development into a specialist role.

## COUNCILLORS, OFFICIALS AND THE PRESS

We have noted above some of the immediate causes of local press performance. The press is, as we have stressed, part of the local political system, and in assessing it we must consider its relationship with the chief actors in the system, the councillors and officials. It is as well to recognise that conflict is inherent in the situation on both sides. Journalists find themselves facing two élites, the political and the bureaucratic, each with an element of conflict built into its relation with the other, and each with its own syndrome of attitudes to the management of news. We may symbolise them by Figure 3.

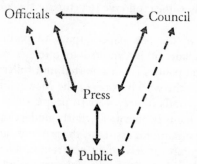

*Figure 3.* (*The strong lines represent a direct relationship; the broken ones an indirect.*)

Councils and councillors themselves must shoulder some of the responsibility for the poor performance of the press. The oligarchic tendency inside the political parties makes journalists' jobs both easier and more difficult. Easier in the sense that some of the key leaders who can make policy may seek to use them by supplying news. Harder in the sense that it is very difficult to unravel the truth behind party positions on key areas of policy when those positions are arrived at secretly and participants in the decisions wish to preserve that secrecy. Our editors all shared perceptions of strong trends towards alderman – senior officer rule, which left councillors, far less voters, outside a perceived 'magic circle'. As Dilys Hill puts it 'Councils are elected to administer local services. As a result they are largely indifferent to demands that they should take the initiative in publicising their work.'[10] Having gone through the elective process, councillors are jealous of their legitimacy and hostile to others – journalists or community activists – who try to 'get in on the act'. As the research on 'The Local Councillor' for the Maud Committee found, councillors believed voters did not know enough to judge issues, yet were ambivalent towards supplying them with more information or using means other than their personal contacts to learn of the needs or views of their voters. Councillors saw the mass media as a useful channel to supply information to voters but were clear, as Dilys Hill found in West Yorkshire, that *they* 'were the main avenue of contact between the citizen and the local authority'.[11]

Local authority chief officers shared this view of the function of the mass media and the role of councillors. More, via N.A.L.G.O., they have pressed hard to increase the supply of information through better public relations activities, sometimes in the face of opposition from councillors. 'The union', as Dilys Hill puts it 'considers that it continues to be the leader in this drive, with the local authorities as very much the followers, albeit enthusiastic ones once they become convinced of the efficacy of such work.'[12]

The attitudes of both councillors and officers stress 'the hierarchic nature of the representative system'.[13] Both enjoy their monopoly of being 'in the know', and generally are aware of the benefits of the absence of probing by well-informed and equipped journalists. The N.A.L.G.O. attitude to public relations work is frankly managerial and councillors have come to share this. Dilys Hill quotes Mr Laurence Evans, formerly at the Local Government Information Service, saying that while there will always be some conflict between the press, 'jealous of its freedom', and the executive, the Information Officer 'should be a bridge between the local council and their officers and the press and the public . . . [he can] . . . help establish working relationship'.[14] Bridges, however, are meant to be crossed both ways and, given councillor and officer attitudes, the working relationship is likely to be understood as better management of journalists and the public alike.

When councillors and officials complain of press coverage it is on the ground of misreporting, basic lack of understanding, triviality, lack of publicity for public spirited work being done. Many would not welcome a service which remedied these deficiencies but was also able to uncover inefficiencies, intra-party dissensions or corrupt practices. If such a style of reporting were to emerge, news management would become as much a problem for Town Hall as for the local press. The continuance of the present situation is, therefore, not a bad bargain for many in the political leadership.

The ideal Town Hall view of political reporting was given to us by Liverpool's City Publicity Officer. In 1965 Liverpool had appointed its own public relations officer, with a brief to improve the city's image in the country at large and abroad. This move was not designed primarily to improve local communication and, during the period under review, had little discernible effect locally. Yet in 1971 the City Publicity Officer, as he was now called, did feel the need to respond to the inadequacy of press coverage of such city matters as planning, health, environment, neighbourhood participation. He began his own highly professional (he had formerly been a journalist in another provincial town) eight-page tabloid, which was distributed free to all households and was intended to appear twice a year. Ideally, he would have liked to be able to produce this quarterly.

Clearly, the problem as the City Publicity Officer saw it was a problem of the management of information. As a part-insider in both the press and the local government worlds, his view was far from simple. He felt the public should have more information, but not just random information. He was not against a campaigning press, but it must be constructive. The Liverpool papers did not 'knock' the local government, he acknowledged, but he was tired of local government being lampooned, or ignored altogether. He would have agreed with John Whale that too much press attention is given to the trivial. He would have approved of Whale's example of local press coverage; a long meeting of Weston-super-Mare's Finance and General Purposes Committee in which 49 minutes were passed but only two received mention, namely, a staff social club ('Civil Servants' rest room' was the headline) and a lavatory for the Information Bureau ('It's such a relief').[15]

With the pressures, then, on all sides, towards 'news management', any commentator with an interest in the health of local democracy must insist on the importance of the public having as many alternative sources of information as possible, not only through the established local press but elsewhere as well.

NEWSPAPERS, BUSINESSES, AND THE 'GOOD OF THE TOWN'

Let us turn now to consider the local newspaper as a profit-making organisation; for the point is worth reiterating that while newspapers are in business to serve a number of ends, the chief thing about them is that they are in business. Banfield and Wilson put it thus

The metropolitan daily newspaper is one of the very few actors on the civic scene . . . in a position both to take a comprehensive view of the public interest and to exercise a powerful influence upon all of the other actors. It is, therefore, a political institution of great importance. But it is also a business – a manufacturing company which must meet a payroll and return dividends to stockholders. To understand its civic role, one must keep these two functions in mind and be aware of the tension that exists between them.[16]

There are local papers where proprietorial interest lies as much in influence as in profit. There are those, like the *Liverpool Weekly News*, where it is clear that a crusading political position is an attractive selling line, though not the less sincerely held for that. In the case of the other five newspapers studied, however, it is hard to detect any sustained effort 'to exercise a powerful influence' upon the other actors in the civic scene. Much of the time there has been little discernible consistent political stance at all. Certainly, nothing to lead one to suspect a Beaverbrook or a Harmsworth behind the scenes. We are impelled, therefore, to give attention to the business aspect of the local newspapers' role and to doubt whether, in Britain, anything like a tension exists, even in theory, between this and the political role.

The business nature of the local press affects their performance in two respects. Firstly within the newspaper organisation itself, an awareness of the costs and benefits of putting effort into different kinds of coverage militates against investigatory and interpretative political journalism. This would almost certainly cost vastly more than, say, the addition of a nationally syndicated gardening column, in return for a probable loss rather than gain in readership. Again, where newspapers are part of a chain, the central management will be under a strong economic impulse to put in to any one newspaper no more staff and especially no more senior staff than are absolutely necessary for viable operations. This was clearly the case with the weekly papers of the *Post* and *Echo* Group. The incentive to put an effort into higher quality political reporting would have to come from outside the present structure of local newspaper management. Editors tend to think that they are already more than doing their duty by local government, which they often perceive as a dull area punctuated by occasional melodrama (though this could apply equally to the bulk of the rest of their material). They will give more detailed news, and news of neighbourhood concern, only if it fits into their perceptions of what the readership in aggregate will take. They are entrepreneurs dealing in news. Political news, like other sorts of news, is raw material for filling space. Journalists have evolved and internalised sets of criteria for deciding how much of it to use and what sorts of treatment to give it – what, in short, is newsworthy. There are comparatively few payoffs, from their point of view, in the effort of going outside well-worn routines. The weekly press's circulation can only move within fixed limits, and the contribution that a bigger and better editorial staffing effort could make towards increasing it would be unlikely to gain much reward in increased advertising revenues. For advertising revenue is the life-blood of the newspaper as a business. Writing of the national media, John Whale argues that though they have retained their freedom as actors 'the need for advertising has increased the tendency in news organisation to assimilate their standards to those of the money making classes'.[17] He notes how, among the London dailies, the paper most well-spoken of by journalists on the other papers is the *Financial Times*. 'It cannot', he concludes, 'be altogether an accident that the *Financial Times* is the only one of the eight with a body of readers for whose attention it has in effect no competition.'[18] What is necessary is not the pursuit of extra circulation as such, but to keep advertising revenue flowing in. And here, the paper has a direct, vested interest in the wellbeing of the town's economy.

This is, of course, the second element. As a business itself, and one dependent on the support of other local businesses, there is every reason for the paper, from both predilection and calculation, to view the continued and enhanced prosperity of the town, as defined by local businessmen, to be the supreme good. As we have seen, editors were much concerned with the 'image' of their towns; their concern about industrial relations had little to do with an interest in the rights and wrongs of particular cases or with the structure of industrial organisation but much to do with the effects on local 'prosperity' of bad publicity. This in turn subsumed the newspaper's concern for *its* prosperity as a business. This, dependent as it is on advertisements, is acutely sensitive to economic 'downturns'. John Whale noted of the chorus of national newspaper demands for reflation in 1971 that 'thunderous leading articles in favour of expansion were not dictated by patriotism alone'.[19] Similarly, the problems associated with bad housing and poverty got comparatively little attention, and some questions such as colour relations were ignored altogether. Of the local weekly papers, Banfield and Wilson noted in America that 'their social functions, which they more or less consciously pursue, is that of creating a sense of community by stressing matters that are noncontroversial and of common interest in the locality'.[20] While not the whole story on Merseyside, we would certainly confirm this as perhaps the most powerful political inclination of the weeklies, not excluding the *Liverpool Weekly News*, whose one class readership and distance from the city's establishment allowed it a different variation on the theme.

The nature of the present news-gathering process completes the process outlined above. The weekly press, being undermanned and underspecialised, relies on clichés and consensus for its political opinions, and on official handouts and verbatim reports for its news. Hence the overwhelming weight of news coverage will be of the Town Hall point of view, its arguments will be well set out, at least in comparison with anyone else's, and the paper will naturally be very likely to endorse them.

The entire syndrome of press attitudes to the 'good of the town', the essential sympathy towards the 'official' point of view, is illustrated in a recent study of the planning process in Newcastle upon Tyne.[21] The main burden of this study is that comprehensive planning was entered into with burning zeal for the future but scant regard for the wishes of those about to be planned; that the tools the planners used to carry out their mission were grossly inadequate and that its main result was blight, and paralysis of a neighbourhood. The Newcastle papers published criticisms, but their own attitude was enthusiastic. Mr Burns, the chief planning officer, was, *The Journal* told its readers in November 1967, 'a man of faith, and it needs the politician and rate-paying Novocastrian to see the future through his eyes if it is to come true'.[22]

Like most business organisations, too, the local press has seen an increasing tendency to bureaucratisation and to a loss of distinctiveness. Of the six papers studied here, five were part of one business. C. P. Scott remarked in 1921 that 'It is much to control one newspaper well; it is perhaps beyond the reach of any man, or any body of men, to control half a dozen with equal success.'[23] Certainly, the Merseyside paper with the most vigorous personality of its own was the only independent one. But that in itself is less important than the suspicion that in the case of the majority the balance to which Scott drew attention between the 'material' and 'moral' existence of a paper has been weighted firmly on the side of the former.

Another factor making for weaker service to the public is, in some cases, that circulation areas are dictated by past business history and are often ill-related to the areas that are meaningful in terms of people's perceptions. The Liverpool dailies have to divide their attention between a range of different local authority areas, thus weakening the impact of coverage of any one individual authority. Jones reports that this is also the case in Wolverhampton and no doubt it is true in many other areas. On the face of it papers which spread their coverage over a wider population give poorer coverage than those dealing with smaller areas. Given the area covered by the Liverpool dailies and their commitment to include coverage of national and international news as well as local news, we might suggest that Liverpool people are less well served for local news, despite there being two daily papers, than are the people of Bootle with their weekly. In the former, journalists are aware that they can only give news of importance to one relatively small locality if it can be justified in terms of appeal to readers spread over a very wide area.

The reorganised local government system operational from 1973–1974 will produce a situation in the metropolitan areas in which the pattern of local newspaper coverage and circulation will bear a closer relationship than before to the local government pattern. The difference between matters of concern locally, such as the administration of basic services, and those of concern to the whole conurbation, such as strategic planning and transportation, which, broadly, has been reflected in the different foci of the weekly and the conurban daily, will be institutionalised in the two tiers of local government. In the case of Merseyside this will mean one top tier authority for the conurbation and four district authorities, Liverpool being one, one being based on a number of towns on the eastern side of the conurbation, and two, significantly, covering very largely the same areas as are now served by the West Cheshire Group of Newspapers (including Birkenhead and Wallasey) and the Southport Visiter group (including Bootle). In the latter cases what changes in newspaper organisation, if any, are likely to ensue is uncertain, but it is obvious that a greater concentration of effort on political and local government reporting now becomes possible. That part of the new metropolitan area served by West Cheshire Newspapers will have one distinct authority where hitherto it has had five. Chains of weeklies in other areas of the country will have similar opportunities.

THE NEW COMMUNITY PRESS

The research for the Redcliffe–Maud Commission[24] revealed that the areas that have most meaning for people tend to be comparatively small neighbourhoods, defined by such communal institutions as churches, schools, shopping centres, public houses. It is at this level that most of what local government provides assumes reality in most people's lives. Emerging from these levels we have begun to see in recent years the appearance of an undergrowth of 'community papers'. These have taken advantage of the offset lithographic printing technique which is particularly suited to this type of publishing. For an admitted variety of motives, groups of people in particular situations have been working to raise consciousness of certain issues. They aim to be particular where the established local press insists on being general.

The growth of an 'alternative' press on Merseyside post-dated the period covered in this study. Most of the organs comprising it started up in 1970 and later, making use of the advantages of photolithographic production. In many respects the papers have a remarkably similar character. All those which successfully established themselves reached settled circulations at between 2,500 and 5,000.

All have a campaigning, populistic stance. Their worlds are full of 'enemies of the people' such as landlords or 'bureaucrats'. They go in for rousing, indeed even screaming, headlines. And they are often laid out and written with considerable skill. In one case, the *Liverpool Free Press*, this is not surprising since the writers were largely people with a journalistic background. Their product was well laid out, with clever use of graphics, and showing all the marks of having been written by informed people with a good network of contacts. Attacks on the *Post* and the *Echo* were a frequent feature. The paper's masthead motto was 'News you're not supposed to know'. Others were established by political and religious organisations doing social work in certain areas. One, the *Toxteth People* later *Mersey People*, was overtly party political, being a brave attempt on the part of the Toxteth Constituency Labour Party. It failed. The most notable achievement, however, was that of the *Tuebrook Bugle*, a twelve-page monthly started in February 1971, written, as it asserts on its masthead, 'by the people for the people'. This effort, initiated by a group of housewives in an area of East Liverpool, campaigned with some success for the kind of amenity improvements which mean a lot to a particular district but get little publicity, or perhaps consideration, in the welter of problems of a city of well over half a million people. Significantly, frustration at local inability to get local grievances aired in the *Post* and the *Echo* was a key factor in the initiation of this paper.

Comment is free. And in making it, the new community press proclaims the existence of felt needs for a kind of press coverage which the established local press has manifestly failed to provide. This is a welcome development in that it is part of a movement towards the opening up of local political debate. From the grass roots, the big city daily like the *Liverpool Post* and the *Liverpool Echo* is often seen, not without justification, as simply another part of 'down town' like the Town Hall and the big business firms. Various allegations are made about the connections between the latter and the newspaper organisation. The truth of these hardly matters. But there is validity in the accusation that the established press often appears from its output to be in all too comfortable a relationship to the powers that be.

The growth of the local 'alternative' press is often seen, on both sides, as a challenge to the pretensions of the existing big city newspaper. Certainly, if the latter's inadequacies of reportage, and its basic position as a component part of the business world, are thrown into focus, so much the better. Yet the dichotomy is a false one. The provincial daily cannot cover the affairs of local neighbourhoods in any depth, any more than the national press can give more than sporadic coverage of events in any one city (unless that city is a Belfast). The press network of the country is rather like a set of Chinese boxes,[25] each smaller than the other, and ranging from the Fleet Street based nationals, through the provincial morning and evening dailies to the local weeklies. There is room for a valuable smaller box at neighbourhood level. This is particularly so in the large cities which, London apart, do not have the benefit of a weekly or bi-weekly with a more restricted focus than that of the dailies. At this local level also there is an opportunity for journalistic activity which does not require the finance or personnel of a larger scale operation and can be done by 'amateurs'. This being so we may expect such a press to continue to grow, especially as publishing and distribution techniques are evolved suitable to the scale of activity; though it would hardly be surprising if many of the papers themselves showed a history of rapid emergences and failures.

THE FLOW OF NEWS: MEANS OF IMPROVEMENT?

The relationship of the local newspapers to communities is, then, fraught with peculiar difficulties. As businesses, it is too much to expect them to surmount these alone. We believe that there is no reason why they should not adopt a more lively and enquiring stance within present resource limitations than they do at present. But there also needs to be a change of attitudes and arrangements on the part of the council. Where the council has a facility such as a press office (whatever its title) it should be to help the press pursue investigations and enquiries rather than as part of a public relations exercise – which tends to be the case at present. It would be as well if the officer in charge of this office were not an employee of the council, as he can hardly be expected to bite the hand that feeds him. If a system of local ombudsmen were to come about, he could, perhaps, be linked with that organisation.

One area of potentiality for reform lies in the strengthening of the Thatcher Act. The press, urges Roger Burke,[26] should be enabled to attend council meetings and committee meetings as of right; all exclusions of the press should be given public justification, unless the justification itself would be prejudicial to the matter in question (there is a great let-out for a secretive authority here); and there should be effective sanctions for offending local authorities. Young journalists should undergo training courses where they would meet key councillors and officials, and the Local Government Information Office would furnish journalists with a manual on local government functions, statistics etc. We would not disagree, but doubt whether these measures would really make much difference. There is at present little evidence that the use of background briefings, admission of press to committees (where permitted), informal press conferences and the other devices recommended by the Local Government Information Office makes much difference to what appears on the printed page, since it may simply mean access to more of the same sort of material as before. The press clearly lacks the incentive and the staff to profit fully from the increased opportunities. Any recommendations must tackle the basic questions of incentive for the papers to adopt different attitudes to reporting and their lack of resources, in many cases, to do it with. The latter is especially the case with the four weeklies covered in this study. Staffed by a handful of men each, none of them could claim to be local government specialists, having neither the time nor the need, strictly speaking, to build up the network of contacts in and around the Town Hall that would be a necessary precondition for a break-away from reliance on reports, handouts and verbatim chunks of council minutes.

One way, perhaps the only way, to break away from this situation is to develop a local equivalent of the national lobby-correspondent/ political columnist system. Reporters with equivalent labels are, of course, used by the big provincial dailies; it would be wrong to say that no progress in this direction has been made.

But to call a reporter a municipal affairs correspondent, and to give him a by-line, does not *make* him one, in any serious sense. Such a correspondent would have to have time to get to know politicians (and officials) personally, and to study general trends and developments in local government and city affairs across the country. He would thus be able to report, as the Westminster political correspondent does, from a base of a network of his own contacts and with authority based on wide knowledge of the system and its problems. George Jones reports that in Wolverhampton for most of the period from the 1900s to the 1950s one reporter 'concentrated completely on the affairs of the Town Council and got to know intimately the local officials and politicians'.[27] The local paper as a source for the study of local politics, says Jones, is much more valuable for the period before 1914 than today.

The reporter of sixty years ago was not so dependent on the Council for official handouts and press releases as he is today. Then he would have to do much digging out of stories himself, but today with the pressure of work so much more intense, he is grateful to the Council for predigesting so much of his material.[28]

It would be an error of perception to urge, *tout court*, that the local newspaper ought to model its reportage of politics more on that of the national newspapers. Local government is not central government in miniature. Moreover, the picture of what goes on in Westminster which is given by Fleet Street is itself misleading. The Parliamentary scene which the national press describes may be the contemporary equivalent of the outward show which masks the hidden realities of political power that Bagehot, 100 years ago, saw as the essence of the English constitution. There is a tendency for political reporters to give a picture of an endless cricket match with the 'ins' batting to the bowling of the 'outs'. While this is undoubtedly an aspect of politics, much, and perhaps the crucial part, of the structure of power at central level is located in quarters which are removed from direct press scrutiny. This is true of the operations of Whitehall, where what Lord Francis-Williams called the 'plague of secrecy'[29] achieved its most notable, though not sole, success when the *Sunday Times* had to withdraw its appointment of Mr Anthony Howard as a 'Whitehall correspondent'. It is also true of Parliament itself, where much of the real work of government takes place in inner party committees and parliamentary committees behind doors closed to the press. Despite this, the corps of Westminster lobby correspondents do manage to convey to their readers a good deal more of the essence of what is happening than local readers will learn of Town Hall; while the national press is also able to back this service up with a corps of high-prestige political columnists whose 'think-pieces' have become an almost indispensable part of national political debate.

The larger provincial paper employs a municipal correspondent; but he is not used in the above way. He is a reporter, not a correspondent. Much of what he writes is the local political equivalent of 'man bites dog'. He does not do much research and he does not write 'think-pieces'. With the smaller papers, of course, it is quite out of the question. If we are to take seriously the need to improve local political knowledge and debate, we ought to consider means of providing incentives to the local press to employ proper local government political correspondents. Where weekly papers are concerned, advantage might be taken of the fact that many of them are already in area-wide groupings, as is the case of the Merseyside local weekly papers. One correspondent serving the group as a whole would have an economically viable role where each paper on its own could not possibly employ him. This is a possible position since what is needed is not more reportage of specific events but general discussion of their significance in the light of local government trends and community changes.

For such a development to come about there would need to be government intervention to give the press material encouragement. A tax incentive to publishers employing such staff might be one possibility.

As a quid pro quo for greater openness on the part of local authorities to the kind of probing involved in this kind of journalism, they have, of course, a right to expect journalists to observe a recognised code of conduct. Respect for confidences, careful checking of facts, and restraint from sensationalism. Respect, too, for the fact that local politicians are not professionals pursuing public careers, but voluntary unpaid private citizens. In turn, however, the councillors and officials might hope to be reported with more understanding and less triviality, and ultimately to enjoy a better informed citizen body.

In any event, the responsibility for improving our channels of political communication lies not with the press alone, or with the local authorities, but with the polity as a whole.

If we believe that the renewal of local government should also be the occasion of the renewal of local democracy, we will think the effort worthwhile.

# Notes

CHAPTER I

1 *Committee on the Management of Local Government* (Maud Report) (H.M.S.O. 1967, vol. 3, pp. 22–9).
2 *Report of the Committee on Public Participation in Planning* (Skeffington Report) (H.M.S.O. 1969), Paras. 104–14.
3 Maud Report, vol. 2, pp. 230–5.
4 *Ibid.* p. 235.
5 A. H. Birch, *Small Town Politics* (London, O.U.P. 1959).
6 F. Bealey *et al.*, *Constituency Politics* (London, Faber, 1965).
7 W. Hampton, *Democracy and Community* (London, O.U.P. 1970).
8 R. Rose, *Influencing Voters: a Study of Campaign Rationality* (London, Faber, 1967).
9 J. Trenaman and D. McQuail, *Television and the Political Image: A Study of the Impact of Television on the 1959 General Election* (London, Methuen, 1961).
10 C. Seymour-Ure, *The Press, Politics and the Public* (London, Methuen, 1968).
11 Ian Jackson, *The Provincial Press and the Community* (Manchester U.P., 1972).

CHAPTER 2

1 Source: *Press Council Annual Reports.*
2 C. Seymour-Ure, *The Press, Politics and the Public* (London, Methuen, 1968); see chapter 2 *passim.*
3 Ian Jackson, *The Provincial Press and the Community* (Manchester U.P., 1972), pp. 34–8.
4 Source: *Editorial Manpower in the Provincial Newspaper Industry* (National Union of Journalists. Mimeo 1969). Exact figures cannot be given since this information is based on a survey to which a high proportion, but not all, newspapers replied, and not all the data is broken down between dailies and weeklies.
5 Jackson, *op. cit.* pp. 24–5.
6 In E. Moonman (ed.), *The Press, a Case for Commitment* (Fabian Society Tract No. 391, March 1969).
7 Dilys Hill, 'Democracy in Local Government – A Study in Local Government' (University of Leeds, Ph.D. thesis, 1966), p. 204.
8 The statistical basis upon which advertisers plan is the cost of reaching 1,000 readers.
9 John Goulden, *Newspaper Management* (London, Heinemann, 1967), p. 56.
10 *Ibid.* p. 57.
11 *Ibid.* p. 59.
12 D. McQuail, *Toward a Sociology of Mass Communications* (London, Collier–Macmillan, 1969), p. 10.

13 Hill, *op. cit.* p. 239. She found this in West Yorkshire.
14 *Ibid.* p. 209.
15 *Ibid.* p. 210.
16 Alan Beith 'The Press and English Local Authorities' (Oxford University, B.Litt. thesis, 1968), p. 148.
17 For a full discussion of the Act see Beith, *op. cit.* pp. 20–35, 47–50.
18 *Committee on the Management of Local Government* (H.M.S.O., 1968), vol. 5, tables 1 and 50a.
19 *Circular* 21/61.
20 Quoted in Roger Burke, *The Murky Cloak: Local Authority Press Relations* (London, Charles Knight, 1970), p. 71.
21 *Committee on the Management of Local Government*, vol. 5, table 2.
22 Beith, *op. cit.* p. 46.
23 Hill, *op. cit.* pp. 226–7.

CHAPTER 3

1 K. Deutsch, *The Nerves of Government* (Glencoe, Free Press, 1963).
2 R. Rose, *Politics in England* (London, Faber, 1965).
3 D. Butler and D. Stokes, *Political Change in Britain* (London, Macmillan, 1969), p. 244.
4 H. Lasswell, 'The Structure and Function of Communication in Society', in L. Bryson (ed.), *The Communication of Ideas* (N.Y., Harper, 1948).
5 R. Merton and P. Lazarsfeld, 'Mass Communication, Popular Taste, and Organised Social Action' in Bryson, *op. cit.*, p. 98.
6 Charles R. Wright, 'Functional Analysis and Mass Communication', *Public Opinion Quarterly* 24 (1960), 605–20.
7 B. Berelson, 'What "Missing the Newspaper" means', in P. Lazarsfeld and F. Stanton, *Communication Research 1948–49* (N.Y., Harper, 1949), pp. 111–29.
8 M. Schraum, quoted by D. McQuail, *Towards a Sociology of Mass Communications* (Macmillan, London, 1969).
9 See C. Seymour-Ure, *The Press, Politics and the Public* (London, Methuen, 1968), chapter 2 for a discussion of this evidence.
10 R. V. Clements, *Local Notables and the City Council* (London, Methuen, 1969), pp. 44–5.
11 See e.g. H. Himmelweit, 'A Theoretical Framework for the Effect of Television. A British Report, *Journal of Social Issues*, 18, no. 2 (1962), 16–29.
12 D. Eutler and D. Stokes, *op. cit.* pp. 225–6.
13 Quoted in Lord Francis-Williams, *The Right to Know* (London, Longmans, 1969), p. 2.
14 Economist Intelligence Unit, *The National Newspaper Industry* (London 1966).
15 W. Breed, 'Social Control in the Newsroom', *Social Forces*, 33 (1955), 326–35. See also A. Metejko, 'The Newspaper Staff as a Social System', in J. Tunstall (ed.), *Media Sociology* (London, Constable, 1970), pp. 168–80.

16 Source: A. Z. Bass, 'Refining the Gatekeeper Concept', *Journalism Quarterly* 46 (1969), 69–72.
17 D. C. Shaw 'Surveillance versus Constraint', *Journalism Quarterly* 46 (1969), 707–12.
18 In his *Public Opinion* (Macmillan Co., New York, 1922). Quoted in Charles Steinberg (ed.), *Mass Media and Communication* (New York, Hastings, 1966), p. 148
19 J. Galtung and M. Ruge, 'The Structure of Foreign News', in Tunstall, *op. cit.* pp. 259–98.
20 J. D. Halloran et al., *Demonstrations and Communication: a Case Study* (London, Penguin, 1970).
21 P. Whitehead, review in *The Listener*, 6 August 1970.

CHAPTER 4

1 See Kathleen Pickett, 'Merseyside's Population and Social Structure' in R. Lawton and C. M. Cunningham (eds.), *Merseyside: Social and Economic Studies* (Longman, London, 1970). The chapter contains an extensive discussion of demographic change in the conurbation. See pp. 72ff.
2 *Ibid.* p. 74.
3 *Ibid.* p. 94.
4 *Ibid.* pp. 85–9.
5 General Registry Office *Sample Census 1966*, England and Wales, County Report, Lancashire (H.M.S.O. 1967).
6 *Ibid.* Cheshire.
7 *Ibid.* Cheshire.
8 *Ibid.* Lancashire.
9 *Royal Commission on Local Government in England*, vol. 2, *Profile of the Conurbations* (H.M.S.O., 1969).
10 Kathleen Pickett, *op. cit.* p. 119.
11 See, e.g. R. Baxter, 'The Working Class and Labour Politics', *Political Studies*, 20, no. 1 (March 1972), 97–107.
12 See, eg., Noel T. Boaden, *Urban Policy Making* (C.U.P., 1971).
13 *Ibid.* chapter 2, pp. 110 ff.
14 *Ibid.* footnote 3, p. 143.
15 *Newspaper Press Directory*, 1970.
16 O. P. Williams and Charles R. Adrian, *Four Cities* (Philadelphia, University of Pa. Press, 1965), pp. 22–36.

CHAPTER 9

1 Quoted in L. J. Sharpe, 'Theories and Values of Local Government', *Political Studies*, 18, no. 2 (1970), 161.
2 E. C. Banfield and J. Q. Wilson, *City Politics* (Cambridge, Mass., Harvard University Press, 1963), p. 322.
3 *Public Relations and Communication* (London, Local Government Information Office, 1970).

4  Alan Beith, 'The Press and English Local Authorities' (Oxford University, B.Litt. thesis, 1968), p. 94.
5  See chapter 3.
6  Beith, *op. cit.* p. 179.
7  A. S. Edelstein and J. J. Contris, 'The Public View of a Weekly Newspaper's Leadership Role', *Journalism Quarterly* 43 (1966) 17–24.
8  John Whale, *Journalism and Government* (London, Macmillan, 1972), p. 102.
9  Quoted in *The Times*, 16 February 1972.
10  Dilys Hill, *Participating in Local Affairs* (London, Penguin, 1970), p. 135.
11  Dilys Hill, 'Democracy in Local Government: A Study in participation and communication' (Leeds University, Ph.D. thesis, 1966), p. 22.
12  *Ibid.* p. 133.
13  *Ibid.* p. 133.
14  *Ibid.* p. 151.
15  Whale, *op. cit.* p. 53.
16  Banfield and Wilson, *op. cit.* p. 313.
17  Whale, *op. cit.* p. 67.
18  *Ibid.* p. 69.
19  *Ibid.* p. 67.
20  Banfield and Wilson, *op. cit.* p. 315.
21  John Gower Davies, *The Evangelistic Bureaucrat* (London, Tavistock, 1972).
22  Quoted *ibid.* p. 118.
23  *Manchester Guardian*, May 1921.
24  *Royal Commission on Local Government in England*, Report, vol. 3, 1969, pp. 129ff.
25  The metaphor is that of Robert A. Dahl, in *After the Revolution?* (New Haven, Yale University Press, 1970).
26  R. Burke, *The Murky Cloak: Local Authority Press Relations* (London, Charles Knight, 1970), pp. 90–3.
27  G. W. Jones, *Borough Politics* (London, Macmillan, 1969), p. 15.
28  *Ibid.* p. 16.
29  Lord Francis-Williams, *The Right to Know* (London, Longmans). p. 284.

# Select bibliography

### I. MERSEYSIDE

R. Lawton and C. M. Cunningham (eds.), *Merseyside: Social and Economic Studies* (London, Longmans, 1970).

### 2. MASS COMMUNICATIONS

A. Z. Bass, 'Refining the Gate Keeper Concept', *Journalism Quarterly* 46 (1969), 69–72.

W. Breed, 'Social Control in the Newsroom', *Social Forces* 33 (1955), 326–35.

L. Bryson (ed.), *The Communication of Ideas* (Harper, New York, 1948).

L. A. Dexter and D. M. White (eds.), *People, Society and Mass Communications* (Glencoe, Free Press, 1964).

L. Donohew, 'Newspaper Gatekeepers and Forces in the News Channel', *Public Opinion Quarterly* 31 (1967), 61–8.

A. S. Edelstein and J. J. Contris, 'The Public View of a Weekly Newspaper's Leadership Role', *Journalism Quarterly* 43 (1966), 17–24.

J. D. Halloran *et al.*, *Demonstrations and Communication* (London, Penguin, 1970).

H. T. Himmelweit *et al.*, 'A Theoretical Framework for the Consideration of the Effects of Television', *Journal of Social Issues* 18, no. 2 (1962), 16–29.

P. Lazarsfeld and F. Stanton (eds.), *Communication Research 1948–9* (New York, Harper, 1949).

D. McQuail, *Towards a Sociology of Mass Communications* (London, Collier–Macmillan, 1969).

D. C. Shaw, 'Surveillance versus Constraint', *Journalism Quarterly* 46 (1969), 707–12.

J. C. Sim, 'Community Newspaper Leadership. More Real than Apparent', *Journalism Quarterly* 44 (1967), 276–80.

Chas. S. Steinberg (ed.), *Mass Media and Communication* (New York, Hastings, 1965).

J. M. Trenaman and D. McQuail, *Television and the Political Image* (London, Methuen, 1961).

J. Tunstall, *Media Sociology* (London, Constable, 1970).

Chas. R. Wright, 'Functional Analysis and Mass Communication', *Public Opinion Quarterly* 24 (1960), 605–20.

### 3. THE PRESS IN BRITAIN

Alan J. Beith, 'The Press and English Local Authorities' (Oxford Univ. B.Litt. thesis, 1968).

Roger Burke, *The Murky Cloak. Local Authority Press Relations* (London, Charles Knight, 1970).

## Select bibliography

Economist Intelligence Unit, *The National Newspaper Industry* (London 1966).

John Goulden, *Newspaper Management* (London, Heinemann, 1967).

Dilys Hill, 'Democracy in Local Government: A Study in Participation and Communication' (Leeds Univ. Ph.D. thesis, 1966).

Ian Jackson, *The Provincial Press and the Community* (Manchester U.P., 1972).

E. Moonman (ed.), *The Press, a Case for Commitment* (London, The Fabian Society, Fabian Tract No. 391, March 1969).

Claud Morris, *I Bought a Newspaper* (London, A. Baker, 1963).

The Newspaper Press Directory.

The Press Council Annual Reports, 1971.

*Public Relations and Communication* (Local Gov't. Information Office, London, 1970).

*Royal Commission on the Press*, Cmnd. 1812 (London, H.M.S.O., 1962).

*Royal Commission on the Press*, Cmnd. 7700 (London, H.M.S.O., 1949).

C. Seymour-Ure, *The Press, Politics, and the Public* (London, Methuen, 1968).

John Whale, *Journalism and Government* (London, Macmillan, 1972)

Lord Francis-Williams, *The Right to Know* (London, Longman, 1969).

#### 4. LOCAL POLITICS IN BRITAIN

F. Bealey *et al.*, *Constituency Politics* (London, Faber, 1965).

A. H. Birch, *Small Town Politics* (London, Oxford University Press, 1959).

N. T. Boaden, *Urban Policy Making* (London, Cambridge University Press, 1971).

R. V. Clements, *Local Notables and the City Council* (London, Methuen, 1969).

*Committee on the Management of Local Government*, vols. 1–5 (London, H.M.S.O., 1967).

J. G. Davies, *The Evangelistic Bureaucrat* (London, Tavistock, 1972).

W. Hampton, *Democracy and Community* (London, Oxford University Press, 1970).

D. Hill, *Participating in Local Affairs* (London, Penguin, 1970).

G. W. Jones, *Borough Politics* (London, Macmillan, 1969).

*People and Planning*, Report of Committee on Public Participation in Planning (London, H.M.S.O., 1969).

*Royal Commission on Local Government in England*, Cmnd 4040 (London, H.M.S.O., 1969).

L. J. Sharpe, 'Theories and Values of Local Government', *Political Studies* 18, no. 2 (1970), 153–74.

#### 5. POLITICS, GENERAL

E. C. Banfield and James Q. Wilson, *City Politics* (Cambridge, Mass., Harvard University Press, 1963).

## Select bibliography

D. Butler and D. Stokes, *Political Change in Britain* (London, Macmillan, 1969).

K. Deutsch, *The Nerves of Government* (Glencoe, Free Press, 1963).

D. Easton, *The Political System* (Borzoi Books, New York, 1969).

R. Rose, *Influencing Voters* (London, Faber, 1967).

R. Rose, *Politics in England* (London, Faber, 1965).

O. P. Williams and C. R. Adrian, *Four Cities* (Philadelphia, University of Pennsylvania Press, 1965).

# Index

Banbury 12
Banfield, E. C. (and Wilson, J. Q.) 131, 141, 143
Beith, Alan 12, 14, 132–3
Berelson, B. 23, 24
*Birkenhead News*: circulation 43; contents 51–72 *passim*; on transport 75; on planning 74; on education 76; on ward boundaries 77; general stance 78; on Redcliffe–Maud 102, 104
*Bootle Times Herald*: circulation 43; contents 51–72 *passim*; general stance 86; Bootle 'twinned' 87; on redevelopment 87; on Centenary 88; on housing 89; on education 90; on Redcliffe–Maud 101
Breed, W. 27
Burke, R. 147
Butler, David (and Donald Stokes) 17, 24

children and welfare services 65–66
classified advertisements 9
Clements, R. V. 24
communication: modes 16; social functions of 18; effects of 25
content analysis, methods and problems 47–51
Crossman, Richard, M.P. 13

*Daily Express* 27
*Daily Mail* 27
*Daily Mirror* 24
Defamation Act, 1952 13
Deutsch, Karl 16

Easton, David 21
Economist Intelligence Unit Report (1966) 27
editors: 110–23; on their roles 111; on political news 111–18; on editorials and readers letters 114–16;

on technical change and the future 116–17
education 62
Evans, L. 139
evening newspapers, position of 11
Evening Newspaper Advertising Bureau 6

*Financial Times* 142
Francis-Williams, Lord 149

Galtung, J. (and M. Ruge) 30
Glasgow 5
Glossop 3
Goulden, John 9
Greenwood, Anthony 13, 14

Halloran, J. D. et. al. 32
highways 63–4
Hill, Dilys 9, 12, 14, 139
housing 62–3

Institute of Practitioners in Advertising 6

Jackson, Ian 3
Jeans, Sir Alick 43
Jones, G. W. 148
*Journal, The* (Newcastle-Upon-Tyne) 144
journalists: labour turnover 7–8; socialisation of 27; National Union of 7

Lasswell, Harold 18, 19
Leicester University Centre for Mass Communication 32
Lewin, Kurt 28
Lippman, Walter 29, 30
Liverpool City Publicity Officer 58, 140–1
*Liverpool Daily Post*: circulation 43; contents 51–72 *passim*; editorial contents 53; on bus strike

*Liverpool Daily Post* – contd.
94–5; on education 96–7; on Redcliffe–Maud 100–1
*Liverpool Daily Post and Echo Group* 43, 44
*Liverpool Echo*: circulation 43; contents 51–72 *passim*; editorials 53, 54
*Liverpool Weekly News*: circulation 43; contents 51–72 *passim*; general stance 91; on education 92; on housing 92; on Redcliffe–Maud 101–2
Local Authorities (Admission of Press to Meetings) Act, 1908 13
Local Government Information Office 114

Maud Committee on the Management of Local Government 1
McQuail, Denis 10
Merseyside: conurbation 34; population 35; class and age structure 36; housing density 36; employment in 37–9; politics of 40–3
Merton, R. K. (and Lazarsfeld) 18, 19
morning newspaper 11
municipal correspondent 148–50

Newcastle under Lyme 3
news: creation of 29; advertisements and 55–6; political and news of services 57–8; service coverage 67; 'frequency' of political news 68–70
newspapers: circulation 5; technical change 5; readership 6; chain ownership 8; access to political news 13–14; readers needs 22–24; as organisations 26; in the United States 22–9; in the U.S.S.R. 31

Parsons, Talcott 21
Pierre, Henry 137
planning 63–4
police 65

politicians: on press adequacy 125; on press partisanship 127; on greater access for press 129; on Radio Merseyside 130
press (local): constraints on 135–140; as business 141–7; community press 145; need for better flow of news 147
Public Bodies (Admission of Press to Meetings) Act, 1960 (Thatcher Act) 13
public transport 64–5

Radio Merseyside 44, 130
Redcliffe–Maud, *see* Royal Commission on Local Government
Rose, Richard 16
Royal Commission on Local Government in England and Wales, 1969 99–107
Royal Commission on the Press, 1947–49 14

*Salford City Reporter* 14
Scott, C. P. 1, 144
Sheffield 3
Skeffington Committee 1
*Sunday Times* 149
*Sunday Telegraph* 24

Thatcher Act 13, 147
Thomson, Lord 24
Trenaman, J. (and D. McQuail) 10

Viner, George 8

*Wallasey News*: circulation 43; contents 51–72 *passim*; general stance 78–9, 80, 85; on education 79–81; on transport 83; on ferry service 83; on ward boundaries 84; on Redcliffe–Maud 103, 106
weekly paper 11
Whale, John 137, 140, 142, 143
Williams, O. P. (and Charles Adrian) 44
Wolverhampton 148
Wright, Charles R. 18, 19, 133